Conversations About Politics

Conversations About

POLITICS

Edited by Howard Burton

Ideas Roadshow
INTELLIGENT. INQUISITIVE. INTERNATIONAL.

Ideas Roadshow conversations present a wealth of candid insights from some of the world's leading experts, generated through a focused yet informal setting. They are explicitly designed to give non-specialists a uniquely accessible window into frontline research and scholarship that wouldn't otherwise be encountered through standard lectures and textbooks.

Over 100 Ideas Roadshow conversations have been held since our debut in 2012, covering a wide array of topics across the arts and sciences.

All Ideas Roadshow conversations are available both as part of a collection or as an individual eBook.

See www.ideasroadshow.com for a full listing of all titles.

Contents

Textual Note

The contents of this book are based upon separate filmed conversations with Howard Burton and each of the five featured experts.

Mark Bevir is Professor of Political Science and Director of the Center for British Studies at UC Berkeley This conversation occurred on September 9, 2014.

Jacques Bertrand is Professor of Political Science and Director of the Collaborative Master's Program in Contemporary East and Southeast Asian Studies at the University of Toronto. This conversation occurred on August 20, 2014.

Michael Frazer is Senior Lecturer in Political and Social Theory at the University of East Anglia. This conversation occurred on October 14, 2016.

Josiah Ober is Tsakopoulos-Kounalakis Professor in Honor of Constantine Mitsotakis Professor of Political Science and Classics at Stanford University. This conversation occurred on October 1, 2014.

John Dunn is Emeritus Professor of Political Theory at King's College, Cambridge, and Visiting Professor in the Graduate School of Social Sciences and Humanities at Chiba University, Japan. This conversation occurred on January 14, 2013.

Howard Burton is the creator and host of Ideas Roadshow and was Founding Executive Director of Perimeter Institute for Theoretical Physics.

Preface

One of the most interesting aspects of engaging in informal, long-format conversations with experts is that, if you wait long enough and listen carefully, they are bound to say something that surprises you, something that you haven't thought of before. Of course, in many specialized subject areas this tends to happen quite quickly: even run-of-the-mill insights relayed to us by a cosmologist or neuroscientist or medieval historian have the power to startle anyone who is outside of the field—which invariably means most of us.

But somehow when it comes to politics we all feel differently. Politics, after all, is something that all of us have—to some extent anyway—experienced firsthand: we watch the news, we read the papers, we follow reports on social media, we vote. We have, inevitably, our opinions, our biases. All of which makes it all the more intriguing when we're confronted by starkly different perspectives offered up by political experts that run deeply counter to the unthinkingly imbibed "conventional wisdom".

But it certainly happens. Quite often, in fact.

Like when the UC Berkeley political theorist **Mark Bevir** informs us that the standard left/right bureaucracy/markets divide that the media is continually parroting to us is, in fact, a far cry from what's actually happening in the real world of public policy.

> "I think the idea that we live with a choice between market and state is something that is peddled in the newspapers. What most astonishes me today is that the media—and some academics, I would add—still act as though that's the choice we face. I find that quite astonishing because no set of policymakers, on either the traditional left or the neoliberal right, look at things this way anymore.

"Over the last 20 years, most political institutions in the world have been seeking to spread networks rather than markets or hierarchies. If you just think in American terms, the effect of something like the war in Afghanistan and the evidence that Afghanistan was a failed state led American policymakers to stop thinking in terms of the export of markets, and instead to start thinking in terms of the creation and building up of stable political institutions as a context within which markets might work. Broadly speaking, for 20 years now, the left and the right have begun to converge on the idea that we need more and better-managed networks, rather than either markets or hierarchies.

"There's this kind of emotional attachment to the clarity of an ideological battle that they grew up with that is then blurred once you take seriously the fact that the right actually doesn't believe that strongly in markets anymore, at least not in all contexts. What it's trying to do is build and sustain what it would regard as suitable networks."

Or when University of Toronto political scientist **Jacques Bertrand** points out how Indonesia is a flagrant and often sadly under-recognized example of how Islam is quite compatible with modern democracy.

"The biggest issue I have with media is the underreporting of Southeast Asia in comparison to other regions. Whether it's good news or bad news, you get so few stories, at least if we look at reporting in Europe or North America about Southeast Asia relative to events that are happening in many other regions in the world. We get so much press on the Israeli-Palestinian conflict and many of the failures of the Arab Spring, which is a constant theme that we're finding in the press that continues to reinforce the view that, somehow, there's something fundamentally wrong with Muslim societies.

"And then along comes a democratically, well-run election with very little violence occurring in the world's largest Muslim country and you only get one or two articles that mention it. Now those articles are usually accurate, but the net effect of this imbalance of attention is that it skews perceptions about something as fundamental as the role of Islam in the world today."

Or when University of East Anglia political theorist **Michael Frazer** details how Adam Smith's empathetic urgings are exactly opposite to both our modern image of Smith and our modern image of empathy.

"Too often we think if you empathize with someone you necessarily approve of them: to understand all is to forgive all. And Smith says that it's quite the opposite. That you need to empathetically project yourself into someone's situation in order to judge them, in order to work out what is to be done in that situation.

"And then once you work out what's to be done in that situation, you compare what you would do in that situation, what you feel should be done in that situation, with what that person is actually doing. And if they're doing the wrong thing, then you judge them negatively—not despite, but because of the fact that you've empathized with them, so empathy (or what he called sympathy) is the primary faculty necessary for adequate moral judgement.

"It's interesting: there was actually a controversy a number of years ago when Barack Obama was asked, 'What is the main quality you look for in a Supreme court justice?' and he replied, 'Empathy.' Well, many people were horrified by this, thinking that he was recommending that you shouldn't follow the law but simply going with your gut. But that's exactly the opposite of what I'm talking about here. It's not about going with your first immediate instinct, which may be biased strongly, usually biased strongly in your own favour because you haven't expanded that circle, but maybe biased for, or against, one of the parties in a dispute that you're asked to judge."

Or when Stanford University classicist and political scientist **Josiah Ober** suggests that, however necessary the concepts of equality and freedom are to our sense of a fully-functioning democracy, they fall well short of being sufficient.

"You tend to think about the two big democratic values as being equality and freedom. That's fine. That's a great place to start, as far as I'm concerned. If we're free and equal—at least politically free and politically equal—we're doing pretty well.

"The third value, dignity, sometimes gets sort of 'outsourced' to what is thought of as purely human rights language, and therefore is not strictly considered a part of democracy but rather as part of something that would stand "above" democracy as a kind of basic human right.

"I'm all for human rights, of course; and it's certainly true that a human life does not go as well as it ought to in the absence of dignity. But I also think that dignity is a natural part of a democratic community, because dignity that is only a "human right", independent of a civic community that is sustaining it through the chosen actions of the members of that community, is not likely to actually be preserved."

But perhaps the biggest political surprise of all is offered up by the eminent and caustically straightforward Cambridge political theorist **John Dunn**.

First, he unhesitatingly explodes the all-too-prevalent myth that America's Founding Fathers were dedicated democrats:

"It isn't true that the American Republic was founded on the idea of democracy. The American founders were extremely sceptical of democracy, and they thought it referred to a very bad form of government. And they very actively and militantly argued against allowing anything that would appropriately be described with that word to operate in the United States."

And then he takes careful aim at the entire discipline of political science itself.

"Most academics who work on politics, on political theory, on political philosophy, on political sociology, concentrate on what they think are well-defined questions. And they believe that they provide robust and compelling answers to these well-defined questions. Now, in order to be able to do that with political stuff, you have to pull a long way back from the world. And my general intuitive judgment is that if you pull a long way back from the world of politics, you just lose politics. It's gone.

"And I think that that's definitely wrong. The fact is people do need political comprehension, and the way in which political science has been institutionalized over time is hugely unhelpful—most of it doesn't provide much political comprehension.

*"And even if you take, as it were, all the best bits of it and you somehow juxtaposed them, you don't end up with a very high level of political comprehension because there is no synoptic capability in that juxtaposition, because there is no synoptic **effort**. Nobody tries to answer what, after all, in the end is the primary question, which is, '**What the hell is really going on, and why is it going on?**"*

Strong words. Illuminating words. Surprising words. For all of us. Even political scientists.

How Social Science Creates the World

A conversation with Mark Bevir

Introduction

One of a Kind

There are many disadvantages to being a physicist. The pay is not very good. Breakthroughs are rare. And your colleagues inevitably tend towards the monomaniacal and hyper-competitive. But one unquestionable upside to the whole gig is the opportunity to publicly announce that your professional responsibilities involve discovering the "timeless, all-encompassing laws of the universe".

It is not surprising, then, that physicists tend to overhype that side of things, regularly inventing and casually dropping into conversation such overwrought phrases as *penetrating the mind of God* or *unravelling the secrets of the universe* to triumphantly describe their day jobs.

And it's perhaps equally unsurprising that many non-physicists are led, consciously or unconsciously, to mimic such self-satisfied sentiments, maintaining that they, too, are equally embroiled in a noble quest to bring order to the seeming chaos of their research domains by uncovering the immutable principles and laws that govern their worlds.

So it is that, for well over a century now, there have been untold numbers of anthropologists, political scientists and sociologists who have developed a wide assortment of theories of aggregate human behaviour predicated on the notion of natural social kinds governed by inflexible social science laws that they have claimed to have discovered, or at least refined.

Mark Bevir, though, will have none of it.

Bevir, professor of political science at UC Berkeley and an internationally acclaimed expert in the theory of governance, believes that any attempt to shoehorn political science into a natural science framework is bound to fail.

> *"The type of explanations we want in the social sciences are different. In the natural sciences, when you're engaging with the natural world you're looking at objects which don't have intentionality; whereas when you're looking at human actors, you're looking at objects— people—that clearly do have intentionality, and that we therefore assume are capable of acting for reasons of their own, whether those reasons are conscious, subconscious, or unconscious.*

> *"If we make plans with friends, we assume they will act on reasons. If we think about our own selves and we're making plans for the future, we assume that we are capable of having reasons. We live our lives and we engage with others as though intentionality is the thing to which we must refer to explain actions.*

> *"I think social scientists should therefore explicitly take that into account. And if you do that—if you treat the reasons people have for acting as the causes of their action—then the type of explanation you're going to offer is very different, because you have to appeal to people's reasons; and the best way to understand their reasons is to understand the location of those reasons in the wider web of their beliefs and their desires.*

> *"That kind of explanation, where you're effectively contextualizing— you're making an action intelligible by locating it in the context of a web of beliefs and desires—is very, very different from what we loosely might describe as the search for invariant laws that occurs in the natural sciences."*

Political science, according to Bevir, is therefore an "interpretive art" rather than a science like physics or chemistry is.

Well, fine, you might think. But so what? You can call it whatever you want, but the key question remains: *does it work?* Does political science actually deliver the goods? Does it help us better understand key concepts such as governance, thus moving us down the path towards building more productive, more equitable, societies?

There's the rub. Because Mark believes that correctly appreciating what social science is and does has a direct bearing on our everyday social lives.

In other words, if we adopt the false belief that the social world is composed of some unchanging, fundamental entities on par with atoms or molecules—be they markets or classes or what have you— then we will have no means of recognizing, or even describing, what happens when circumstances change and a new social dynamic is created.

That doesn't happen in physics, of course. Once you know the laws, there's only so much that can possibly happen. And if you discover something else, then you have to go back and revise or extend your laws.

But in a world where possibilities are not governed by pre-set laws, where contingency, traditions and social history rule, it's a very different story. And properly appreciating this veritably infinite spectrum of human cultures and societies in which notions such as networks and hierarchies might become embedded lies at the core of the astute political scientist's "interpretive art".

Put another way: this is not simply about how to be a proper political scientist, sitting in one's ivory tower better analyzing and appreciating evolving human circumstances. Because, essentially, the practice of political science itself—in academe, think tanks, or within government departments—in turn directly influences social policy.

*"We're too inclined to think of social science as something that's trying to describe and explain the world as it is. Often, a better way of thinking about social science is as something that **creates** the world.*

"I think most social scientists find the idea that social science creates the world very surprising. But if you stop and think for a minute, it's blindingly obvious; because every time an idea from the social

sciences finds its way into the policymaking world and policymakers act on it—whether it's Keynesian ideas about economics, or monetarist ideas about the money supply, or network ideas about network governance—whichever it is, once the idea makes its way from the social scientific community into the policymaking world and then inspires a policy, it becomes real."

A different way of looking at things, most assuredly. But this is more than simply a shift in perspective: for Mark, fully appreciating the philosophical underpinnings of political theory carries with it significant behavioural change from the powers that be, not least of which being to directly encourage policymakers to regularly engage with their surrounding community in a spirit of increased dialogue.

"If you are convinced that social science can predict in a law-like way how your citizens are going to behave when you introduce a policy, then you will be convinced ahead of time what the consequences of that policy are going to be.

"But once you reject the idea that social science can tell you that a population is bound to react in a certain way, then you come to think that the way in which the population is going to react is a bit contingent—it depends on the existing beliefs and desires of the population—which are also somewhat consistent but may change through the process.

"In those circumstances, I think policymakers will almost always do well to involve the public—the targets of their policy—in a dialogic process, if only to learn more about how the policy is likely to work out. Even if, after listening to the target group of the policy, we ended up deciding that we definitely did not want to do what they want us to do—even if that's the case, I think the policy will be improved and will be more likely to have the outcomes we wished for if we have been through a dialogic process. The policymakers will be more sensitive to the beliefs and desires of those they think the policy will influence, and, therefore better able to craft and fine-tune the policy so that it fits those beliefs and desires."

So while the jury is still out on whether or not the physicists will ever find the "theory of everything" that can be proudly emblazoned on a T-shirt, social scientists, it seems, are now forced to come to terms with the fact that no such formula, even in principle, can properly underly their research effort.

That's the bad news, perhaps. On the other hand, there is considerable consolation, I imagine, to being able to trumpet the fact that they actually get to create their own world.

After all, reading the mind of God is one thing. Playing God is quite another. And naturally requires an even greater sense of responsibility.

The Conversation

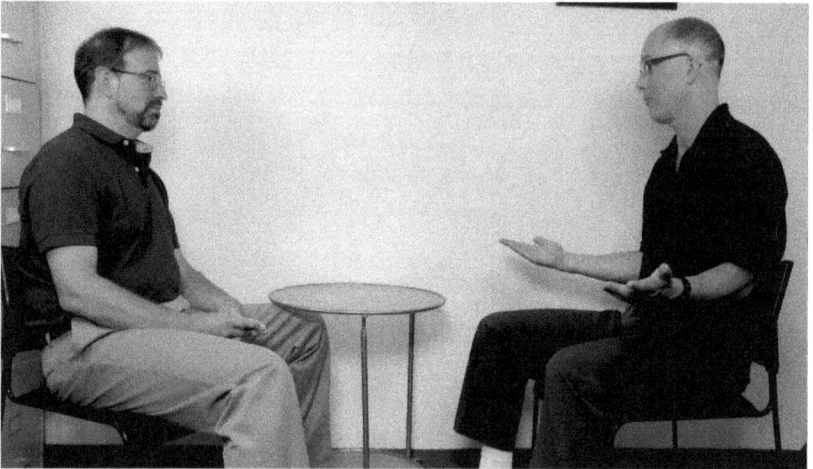

I. Creating a Political Philosopher

From mathematics to social science

HB: I'd like to ask you about your PhD thesis, which was on British socialism. My understanding is that you had a somewhat different take on it, insofar as you weren't somebody who was terribly motivated to look at things in terms of class struggle and class structure.

MB: Yes.

HB: My sense is that you were more interested in individuals and narratives. As I understand it, you started focusing on the historical roots of British socialism and you started breaking out of the standard box-like structures that people typically used when discussing these things at that time.

MB: Yes.

HB: Did that happen as you were doing your studies, or did you go into it with that particular attitude? How did that awareness of looking at things from a broader, more individualistic perspective develop for you?

MB: It's often very hard to be fully self-aware when answering questions like those. I grew up in a family—particular in terms of my mother's influence—which was influenced by Romantic ideas and ideas of self-expression; and probably lurking there was a sense of individual agency and its relevance and importance: not as a formal, academic idea, but as that kind of loose, cultural idea that one inherits from one's family.

When I went to Oxford to do my PhD, I wouldn't say I was self-consciously aware of what you just said, no. I would say instead that I approached British socialism as someone who was more or less self-consciously doing something like political theory, and therefore, the history of political thought.

You're loosely right to say that I adopted an innovative approach. I think someone like Gareth Stedman Jones was also doing something very similar already. So you're loosely right, but I don't think that means that I was doing something extremely innovative.

It's more that, as a historian of political thought, I was naturally interested in what people had said and written; and because the history of political thought tends to go from canonical thinker to canonical thinker, I naturally tended to think about what individuals had written and said. Whereas, at the time—with the exception of someone like Gareth Stedman Jones—the dominant approach to the history of socialism was heavily rooted in labour history and social history, and therefore, it was about the objective characteristics of various types of social movements, or groups of people, around ideas like class.

So although there was this kind of subconscious element of family inheritance, it was really almost just an accident of my wanting to explore British socialism, but wanting to do so as a historian of political thought, rather than a social historian.

HB: Why British socialism in particular? What was it about that that naturally appealed to you?

MB: This was during the Thatcher years. I started at Oxford in 1982 when Thatcher had been around for three or four years, and I was a fairly committed socialist, as long as we understand that term very broadly.

HB: I see that you're sensitive about that because you live in the United States now—you're worried that people might start hurling rocks at you when you use the word 'socialist'.

MB: Yes, but also that New Labour made 'socialist' in many ways a negative term, while Old Labour made it so that the term 'socialist' was heavily associated with things like public ownership and labour politics, all of which I'm much more ambiguous about.

My form of socialism is much more utopian—I don't like the word 'utopian' because it suggests something unrealistic—but what I had in mind was much more idealistic, much more about non-governmental institutions and radical self-rule.

So Thatcher had come to power and, around Thatcher, there were questions about what the state should be and what it shouldn't be. She was very hostile to the state. Moreover, she was branding socialists as 'statists'. I was not so hostile to the state, and, insofar as I was, it was for none of the reasons that she was hostile to the state. I thought of myself as a socialist, but not really a statist.

What I wanted to do was explore socialist ideas about the state and offer an alternative account of socialism to that which I felt was not only being used by Thatcher to caricature socialism but to some extent had been adopted by Old Labour as well, centered around things like collective ownership of the means of production and trade union struggle, rather than about trying to create alternative ways of life.

One of the things that I sometimes tell my students in this context is that slightly after I started my PhD, Ken Livingstone was in charge of the Greater London County Council—

HB: This is 'Red Ken', right?

MB: "Red Ken", exactly.

And that's what he was known as because he was regarded as so off-the-wall left wing. And the kinds of things he did to be labeled "Red Ken" was providing funding for lesbian feminist groups, not his views on nationalization or the like—that wasn't viewed at the time as so desperately crazy and off the wall.

But what was regarded as crazy was this idea that socialism was about alternative ways of being, greater tolerance towards different sexualities, and so forth. I was really sympathetic to all of those things, but not only were they things that were being written out of socialism by Thatcher, they were things that were very marginal within the Labour Party at the time.

HB: Presumably that's also a sign of the willingness of the press, or society at large, to put people into boxes and start stereotyping.

MB: Yes.

HB: Getting back to your story. You clearly have a proclivity towards intellectual history and the history of political thought, and while you have emotional reasons to be aligned in this particular direction— you come from a particular culture, you see Margaret Thatcher in power who calls for the summary elimination or reduction of several aspects of the state that you were not terribly happy about—at the same time you also have a more detached interest in approaches to history and the power of ideas themselves, examining under what circumstances certain ideas gain widespread influence. When did that specific intellectual orientation begin for you?

MB: Again, it's something that's hard to be self-conscious about. The British education system is odd. At school, the only thing I really shone at, until at least age 16 or 17, was mathematics. I'm not like several other major political theorists today who were good at every-thing and who were obviously going to go on to be undergraduates at Cambridge and Oxford and shine.

HB: I thought you were going to say something different. I thought you were going to say, *"I'm not like all these other political scientists who can't add."*

MB: No, no. Anyway, I was good at mathematics, but I was useless at anything with my hands, so I couldn't do anything experimental, which ruled out the sciences. For my A levels (the last two years of high school education in the UK) I ended up doing what was called a Double Maths A level. Then I had to find non-science subjects to go with that, and I chose English and history.

When it came time to go to university, maths was still the only thing I was really any good at, although I also did quite well in history. I could have just gone and done maths, and I did think about that, but it seemed a bit dry. So what I thought I would do is something that combined the 'dealing with humans' stuff of English and history, with the maths. I originally enrolled in a psychology program, but then when I found out that was very experimental and involved doing things with rats, I switched to philosophy and political science.

I think the nearest I can come to explaining why I got interested in the philosophical sides of these things is probably that the only thing I've ever been really good at is abstract, conceptual things, whether numbers or ideas. And I think that if you're quite good at something, and you get a lot of positive praise for it, you tend to come back to it. That's probably how I drifted into thinking about these things more philosophically.

Then, when I arrived at Oxford, there was massive prestige around abstract analytic philosophy, and also a lot of really great people working on it there. And that kind of sucked me in.

For a long time, I was doing the work on British socialism alongside work on the philosophy of the social sciences. Then I stopped doing the philosophy of social science bit while I finished my PhD thesis, but once I got a job, I went straight back to the philosophy of social science bit, which became my first book.

So although they had different roots, there was a sense that the two were moving in tandem, forcing me to think about what they said to one another.

Questions for Discussion:

1. To what extent do you think Mark's early experiences with mathematics might have influenced his later views?

2. Who is Gareth Stedman Jones and why did Mark mention him in this chapter?

II. The Power of Philosophy

How to change the world

HB: I'd like to push you a little bit. Because you're British, of course, and you have this self-effacing aspect of your personality that comes to the fore. I remember a phrase in your book, *A Theory of Governance*, where you talk about the importance of adopting a philosophical approach. You make a remark—and I'm paraphrasing here, so I probably won't get this right—that sociologists of science would be wise to take a more philosophical view instead of only limiting themselves to methodology, as seems to be all too often the case.

As an example, you talk about networks and how everyone is talking about them, yet it's not always immediately clear if networks actually exist. They should first pay some attention to the philosophical aspects, to the ontology of these things. What are networks, in fact? Do they really exist?

You're consistently putting philosophical approaches, philosophical analyses, and philosophical perspectives, front and center; and, in fact, implying, if not outwardly stating, that not enough people are doing this in the social sciences. Is that a fair summary?

MB: Yes, that's very fair. There's a lot to say there. Perhaps the first is, "Once a philosopher, always a philosopher." Once you've learned to think in those ways, you can't unlearn them.

HB: OK, but I suspect that it's more than just habit. You actually think that a philosophical approach is superior on some level, right?

MB: Yes. So aside from the fact that once you've learned to think like that, you can't unlearn to think like that, it's also true that I just intellectually believe in the importance of invoking a philosophical approach. I just intellectually believe that we live in a world in which rigour is almost exclusively associated with methodological rigour.

And while there's obviously a degree of conceptual rigour that goes into the methodological rigour: you have to understand what the numbers mean; you have to understand whether there's any degree of significance attached to a correlation once you find it—

HB: And how to do the experiments in the first place, and all that—

MB: Exactly. So there is rigour there, but that's a different thing from conceptual rigour at a more fundamental level where you would ask questions like, *Is the method I'm adopting appropriate to the object I'm looking at? What is the nature of the object I'm looking at? What is the proper explanation of the object I'm looking at?*

For instance, if I drop a pen and ask, *"Why did that pen fall down?"* you would accept an answer like, *"Gravity."* If I suddenly sit down on the floor when we're walking along and you ask, *"Why did you sit on the floor?"* and I respond, *"Gravity,"* you'll think I'm nuts, because you'll expect me to give you a reason which is more akin to the **reason** I have for doing this. So, in everyday language at least, we use rather different ideas about what constitutes an explanation for a purely physical phenomenon—like a pen dropping—on the one hand, and for human action, on the other.

HB: And therefore it makes no sense to start getting out your methodological hardware and start measuring how quickly people are sitting down and all the rest of that sort of thing.

MB: Exactly. So it's obviously important, because it's only by thinking about those philosophical questions that we can decide what kind of methodological rigour we think is appropriate: to what extent, to what ends, and to what forms of explanation. It's important, irrespective of the answers you come up with, that people should be thinking in those terms.

When you look particularly at the social sciences—I think this is a bit less true now than it was ten years ago—but certainly, ten years ago there was a fashion for people adopting multiple types of different methods. You can virtually always do that. You can look at a phenomenon and can cast light on it by, say, producing a formal model of it from deductive, rational choice principles, or by looking at in-depth case studies, or by doing a "large-N statistical analysis" of it. You can take the same phenomenon and look at it in all of these different ways.

There's nothing inherently wrong with that approach, but if you treat each of those different lenses as generating an explanation, the type of explanation that is generated will generally look very different.

If you're offering a model, presumably the explanation is, *This is what happens when people act rationally,* whereas if you're looking at the case studies, you're suggesting that you need to dig deeper to see what people actually were doing on this occasion, precisely because you're a bit sceptical of the idea that there's a formal, universal, rationality that applies to all these different cases. And a statistical analysis would suggest that people act in uniform ways that are patterned, but not ways that are best treated by modelling. Rather, they act in ways that are perhaps understood by their social location or social position.

Each of these different lenses on the same phenomenon suggests a subtly different mode of explanation, and it's not immediately clear that those modes of explanation are compatible with one another. So someone then has to do the philosophical work of making the explanations compatible with one another, and ideally it's going to be the author, but, alas, sometimes not.

HB: Is this idea of taking a more synoptic view—digging deeper, connecting different results, and different spheres with some sort of philosophical backdrop or structure—gaining more credence, in terms of its popularity within the discipline?

MB: No, I don't think so.

HB: Does it vary much from place to place? You mentioned the grand philosophical tradition at Oxford. Can one point to various different places around the world where this sort of approach is more or less popular?

MB: Not so much. The root problem, I think, is the division of higher education into distinct disciplines, in which philosophy is treated as a separate discipline in its own right. I think that's bad both for philosophy and other disciplines; in this case, political science.

That means that philosophers are often not talking directly to people who are engaged in practices—the practice of political science in this case—or perhaps the practice of science. Instead, philosophy has developed a tendency to turn back on itself and reflect overwhelmingly on philosophy. So it has become dominated—again, this is slightly less true over the last five years—but for a long time it was heavily dominated by issues in metaphysics, epistemology, and philosophy of language, all of which are issues that are primarily internal to philosophy, rather than ones that look out to other disciplines.

Meanwhile, if you're in another discipline—like, say, political science— virtually nobody who goes through a PhD program in political science, unless she is a political theorist, will have any training in philosophy at all. Absent that training, she is unlikely to ever be introduced to what it would mean to do the kind of thinking I'm asking for.

HB: So it's a sociological issue.

MB: Yes.

HB: Perhaps if we invented the discipline of "applied philosophy", we'd be better off.

Questions for Discussion:

1. Should more people study philosophy? Why or why not?

2. Does focusing on the "applied nature" of philosophy somehow cheapen its intrinsic value?

III. What is Political Science, Anyway?

Science vs. interpretation

HB: I'm going to move progressively, I hope, from the more abstract to the more applied, but first I want to touch on some ideas of political theory before we start looking at the applications and the ramifications for the real world.

You talked about how political science is not a science; rather, it's an interpretive art, at some level. My understanding of this statement is that,once again, there is a necessary sense of interpreting these different narratives that occur with different people, in different places, under different unique circumstances. The idea of implying that there's some strict, law-like nature to the entire study of what we call politics is just a misguided idea, and it will never work.

Is that reasonable?

MB: That's pretty reasonable. I would qualify the claim that it's not a science, but it depends what you mean by 'science'. In the 18th and 19th centuries, 'science' really just meant a rigorous, intellectual enterprise. The study of politics can definitely be a rigorous, intellectual exercise, and it can also be a rigorous, intellectual exercise that's rooted in the study of facts. In that sense of the word 'science', I don't have a problem with calling it a science.

But there's another sense of the word 'science', where what it would mean to say "political science is a science" would be to say that the same sorts of explanations that work in the natural sciences work in the social sciences, and I think that's wrong.

I think the type of explanations we want in the social sciences are different. In the natural sciences, when you're engaging with the natural world, you're looking at objects which don't have intentionality; whereas when you're looking at human actors, you're looking at objects—people—that clearly do have intentionality and, therefore, are objects that we assume are capable of acting for reasons of their own, whether those reasons are conscious, subconscious, or unconscious.

HB: As opposed to the pen, say, that you were talking about before.

MB: Yes. And I think, in everyday life, we all lead our lives as if the way we explain human actions is by appealing to the conscious, subconscious, or unconscious reasons of the agent.

If we make plans with friends, we assume they will act on reasons. If we think about our own selves and we're making plans for the future, we assume we are capable of having reasons. We live our lives and we engage with others as though intentionality is the thing to which we must refer to explain actions.

I think social scientists should therefore explicitly take that into account. And if you do that—if you treat the reasons people have for acting as the causes of their action—then the type of explanation you're going to offer is very different, because you have to appeal to people's reasons; and the best way to understand their reasons is to understand the location of those reasons in the wider web of their beliefs and their desires.

That kind of explanation, where you're effectively contextualizing—you're making an action intelligible by locating it in the context of a web of beliefs and desires—is very, very different from what we loosely might describe as the search for invariant laws that occurs in the natural sciences.

So it's in that sense that there's a different form of explanation that's at the heart of political science, and that's why I think it's not a science in the second sense of the word 'science'.

That also explains what I mean by saying that political science is an interpretive art, because what I mean is that, to explain human action, we ascribe beliefs and desires to the actor, and that process of ascription—of saying, when someone sits down, *"He did that because he was exhausted, rather than because of gravity"*—is inherently interpretive. You can't open up someone's head and say, *"There's a belief. There's a desire."* Instead, you're always postulating sets of beliefs and desires to explain sets of actions. That, for me, is an interpretive act.

Questions for Discussion:

1. What do you think "political science" will look like in 200 years? Will it be any different?

2. To what extent will we ever be able to understand the intentions and desires of others?

IV. Knowing One's Limits

Distinguishing heuristic utility from a scientific truth

HB: Personally, I think it's very difficult to countenance how anyone can believe that there can be clear, law-like regularities in the human sciences as there are in the natural sciences. Perhaps some of your colleagues believe that, but as a non-specialist with a natural science background, I find that very difficult to believe.

My problem is actually more in the other direction, as it were. It's clear to me that political science is very different from a natural science, because one has to take into account beliefs, desires, intentionality, customs, tradition, language, culture, upbringing and all sorts of other things, to get a reasonably clear understanding as to why groups of people behave in a certain way, let alone why one individual behaves in a certain way.

But it seems to me that the danger of emphasizing this narrative aspect, emphasizing the individual, is that it might lead to a sort of all-out relativism where you can't say anything general about anybody, anywhere, at any time, where you find yourself unable to meaningfully compare different human societies at all, simply being forced to say, *"Well, all people are unique. They all have their own paths, and therefore we can't abstract away and build any sort of even roughly predictive models."* How would you respond to that? Have other people accused you of that?

MB: Let's start with your second question, which is easier. Yes, lots of people ask me a question like that.

So now let's answer it. I have a range of answers.

One answer is that there's a key distinction between abstract concepts that are descriptive and those that are explanatory. If somebody finds that, let's say, 80% of Berkeley professors vote Democrat—

HB: Only 80%?

MB: Oh, I don't know. Perhaps more. But the point is that this statement, assuming that it's true, is just a descriptive fact. Likewise, you could imagine, with less rigour, having a descriptive fact like, *Capitalism arose in the 17th and 18th century*. That's probably true too, at least of British society.

The problem, then, is not with trying to say things abstractly, but rather with imagining that there's one uniquely correct, abstract, descriptive statement, or imagining that the pattern you find is itself an explanation.

I don't have any problem with the idea of coming up with aggregate statements that clump people together and are not about individuals. To pick an example of a term you just used and I use a lot: tradition. That's an aggregate concept that I like. I think people should talk about traditions. I think tradition plays an important descriptive and explanatory role in explaining why people have shared beliefs. So I don't have any intellectual problem with the idea of talking in abstract terms and using abstract concepts.

In other words, there's nothing wrong with using abstract concepts to *describe* common patterns that exist, invoking concepts such as "liberalism" to refer to a certain type of belief system, or "joined-up governance" to describe certain sorts of institutional arrangements. Where I think people go awry is when they treat those abstract concepts not just as describing patterns, but also, themselves, as giving *explanations* of those patterns, such as the claim, "Joined-up governance can be explained by the properties of modern, post-Fordist society."

When you appeal to an abstract concept to do explanatory work, you need to be careful that the abstract concept you're using is one that can be unpacked in terms of intentionality, rather than one that applies straightforwardly to objective phenomena.

HB: It seems that what you're saying is that there are these facts about the world, but one can't justify them as necessarily happening as a result of some law-like structure because of the fact that they happened to have happened in some particular instance.

MB: Yes, that's exactly right.

Another version of the criticism in your second question, which is sometimes thrown at me, would be something like: *the kinds of aggregate concepts that I would allow for, and the kinds of explanations I favour, are incapable of generating policy-relevant knowledge.*

In other words, the claim is that if we want policy-relevant knowledge, we need to operate using more reified concepts, concepts that use reified categories, and do elide individual intentionality in the way I'm unhappy with.

I have some sympathy—I'm not sure how much, but I do have some—for that view. I think there are times when policymakers need to adopt what we might call rough-and-ready generalizations if they're to make decisions. Sometimes you just have to assume that there's a pattern out there that's going to hold if you're going to make an intelligible choice.

But that doesn't imply that you shouldn't have social science models with their own social-science correlations, or that such correlations and models shouldn't play a role in policymaking, but rather that we should instead always remember to think of these models and correlations as rough-and-ready generalizations.

HB: You're fighting against hubris, to a certain extent.

MB: Yes, absolutely. Too many social scientists either ignore the fact that the knowledge they're offering is at best rough-and-ready and an over-simplification, or they pay lip service to that fact without taking it seriously, so they don't actually bother to do any of the work of unpacking their rough-and-ready generalizations.

Likewise, when we switch to look at the policymakers, I think that too many of the policymakers treat these rough-and-ready generalizations as though they are scientific truths rather than as though they might be useful heuristics with which to think about a policy issue.

So I would challenge both ends, if you like, of the policy-expert spectrum: both the expert and the policymaker. I would say that the expert too often acts as though what he's offering is akin to what science is offering, rather than recognizing that it's about intentionality and, therefore, about contingency.

The policymaker, on the other hand, too often takes what's offered as though it's a scientific truth, rather than a heuristic that can be used to illuminate aspects of the particular decision that has to be made, recognizing that, in the end, the decision is going to rest on that particular case and not on a scientific truth revealed by the heuristic.

Questions for Discussion:

1. What does Mark mean, exactly, when he talks of "reified concepts"?

2. Does political science make progress? Why or why not?

V. Missing The Boat

Beyond outdated dichotomies

HB: A concrete example of what we're saying comes to mind—well, to my mind at least. Tell me if I'm off base here. Most people who consider themselves reasonably well-informed citizens are bombarded with this notion that we live in a world where one has to make a choice between the free market—consumerism, personal choice, individual liberty, and so forth—and a more community-oriented perspective where we're responsive to broader, societal issues. In their extreme versions, the latter reduced to a state-controlled system that rigidly enforces equality everywhere, while the other, is libertarianism, where everybody has free choice.

My sense, from reading some of what you've written combined with my own sentiments, is that this is a false dichotomy, an aspect of this pseudo-scientific framework (my words) of supposedly law-like categories that really don't exist, but are instead mere descriptions of tendencies. These hold true, to some extent—it's not as if they have no descriptive power—but to then assume that it's either one thing or the other and there's no possible way that you can go beyond these intransigent categories, misrepresents not only what does exist but also what could exist in the future.

MB: Yes, but I would add to what you've said. I think the idea that we live with a choice between market and state is something that is peddled in the newspapers and it's something—to go back to the beginning of our conversation—that was parallelled and debated at the time of Thatcher, Reagan, and the rise of neoliberalism.

At that time, what you seemed to have was a fairly stark choice between something like the traditional bureaucratic structures of the welfare state, on the one hand, and the kind of markets associated with things like privatization and contracting out on the other, which were promoted by neoliberals. In the 1980s, I think that choice was one that, although it oversimplified, made ideological sense of the public policy debate at the time.

What most astonishes me today is that the media—and some academics, I would add—still act as though that's the choice we face. I find that quite astonishing because no set of policymakers, on either the traditional left or the neoliberal right, look at things this way anymore.

What seems to me, crudely, to have happened is that the neoliberals tried to introduce markets and the markets failed. They occasionally worked, in some areas, but generally, they failed.

HB: Do you mean their quest for completely unregulated markets?

MB: Well, sometimes, when you privatize, what you get is something that's more like an oligopoly. But also, within organizations, they tend to introduce contracting out and market-like mechanisms. Often, we're led to something that would be better understood as packages of organizations all coming together to deliver a service, rather than a straightforward contractual relationship. The market reforms rarely worked. Instead, what you got were networks.

At the same time as this was happening, the left was retreating intellectually from the idea that bureaucracy was a good thing. Indeed, many of the earliest critics of bureaucracy had been from the left who had seen bureaucracies as unresponsive. Instead, the left turned to networks as an appropriate solution to the problems of both bureaucracy and markets.

If you look at the history of something like the New Labour government in Britain, it's really about the spread of networks much more than the spread of markets. Their key phrase was "joined-up governance": building networks across government institutions rather than marketization.

Over the last 20 years, most political institutions in the world have been seeking to spread networks rather than markets or hierarchies. If you just think in American terms, the effect of something like the war in Afghanistan and the evidence that Afghanistan was a failed state led American policymakers to stop thinking in terms of the export of markets, and instead to start thinking in terms of the creation and building up of stable political institutions as a context within which markets might work.

Broadly speaking, for 20 years now, the left and the right have begun to converge on the idea that we need more and better-managed networks, rather than either markets or hierarchies.

HB: But this is not being described by the modern media.

MB: Exactly. I'm on the academic left, so I tend to pick fights with other people on the academic left, because left-wing people are always infighting, but it seems to me that too many people on the left have a vested interest in talking as if we still live in a world of neoliberalism.

HB: What is their vested interest, exactly? Is it just that they've been saying the same thing for so long that they don't want to change their tune?

MB: To some extent, yes, because they grew up in a world in which the right-wing bogeymen were going to spread markets and capitalism everywhere. That's what Marxism told us was going to happen: that capitalism would try to spread itself everywhere. Once the right wing stood up with Thatcher and Reagan and declared, *"We're going to spread markets everywhere,"* then people on the left said, *"Yes! We always knew it, and at last they've come clean."*

So there's this kind of emotional attachment to the clarity of an ideological battle that they grew up with that is then blurred once you take seriously the fact that the right actually doesn't believe that strongly in markets anymore, at least not in all contexts. What it's trying to do is build and sustain what it would regard as suitable networks.

HB: I understand why some of your academic colleagues might feel this way given what you've just said, but why can't the media appreciate this subtlety?

MB: I have no idea. Two reasons spring to mind, but they're both just conjectures.

The first is that, particularly in the Anglophone world, we live in states that are dominated by two-party systems. So it's easy to have a market/hierarchy contrast that fits onto political parties, so that the political rhetoric around the parties matches on to the ideological debate that you seem to be offering people through your media.

The second possible explanation is that networks are really, really messy; and to try to talk about and discuss a world of networks and bring it alive for an audience is very difficult.

HB: But first you have to understand it yourself.

MB: Yes, exactly.

Question for Discussion:

1. Did any part of this chapter surprise you? If so what and why?

VI. Networks

What they are and how they arose

MB: When it comes to networks, there are two main points I'd like to make here.

The first is that, as we've just said, it's about time that people outside the world of scholars working on public administration realize that we live today in a world where the form of organization that policymakers are really trying to promote is networks, not markets or hierarchies.

The second point is that I have an ambiguous attitude towards networks. On the one hand, I do think that networks are, broadly speaking, often—by no means always, but often—a good alternative to not only markets, but also bureaucracy. On the other hand, I think there's something profoundly wrong with the kind of social science that reifies networks, treats them as having intrinsic properties—as though, for instance, networks are bound to lead to greater levels of innovation—and thereby encourages policymakers to adopt networks on the belief that there is some sort of natural scientific-like law, such as, *Adopt networks and you will get more innovation.*

HB: Let's talk a little bit more about these networks, because I don't pretend to understand this idea deeply at all.

Granted that we're now living in a world where networks are a dominant factor—maybe *the* dominant factor—how has that happened? Describe these networks in some detail for me so I can get a clear understanding of what we're actually talking about.

MB: I always find it hard to try and discuss what forms of governance now predominate, because it's not like you can point to something and say in any meaningful way, *"There's a network".*

You can't draw boundaries around a network and say, *"That's what's included in it and that's what's not included,"* unless you do so in an arbitrary way. Therefore, you can't really count them. Which, in turn, means that the firm claim that networks are proliferating is a little bit meaningless.

What I would want to say—and this is just my personal, loose impression of government—is that bureaucracy still remains the predominant pattern of organization within the public sector. But in my lifetime what we've seen is an increasing rise of network-like organizations at the expense of traditional bureaucratic structures. That's, then, my response, to the general question of how I would characterize the public sector.

As for how this happened, I think it happened in two waves. The first wave occurred when people tried to promote markets, when people like Thatcher and Reagan introduced things like contracting out, whereby the public sector, instead of providing a service—like cleaning a building—would instead contract out to get a private sector entity to perform that service and pay the private sector entity to perform that service. When neoliberals introduced contracting out, what they actually did was increase the numbers of organizations involved in providing services, which thereby led to the formation of new networks.

Then, in a second wave starting in the mid-90s, policymakers became convinced not only that networks were spreading as a result of neoliberal reforms, but also that networks were often a good thing that could help to create greater involvement, that they could help to create greater innovation and that could help to overcome some problems of financing. Therefore, there was a wave of attempts across many developed countries to promote things like joined-up governance and whole-of-government approaches. And those tended to consist of the deliberate and conscious construction of networks.

So networks arose first as an unintended consequence of neoliberal reforms, and then were reinforced as a deliberate policy agenda. That's how I think it happened.

Now let's talk a bit about what these networks look like. Imagine we go back to 1979—when Thatcher was first elected—and we live in a society with a fairly strong welfare state, and we're interested in the old-age care of our parent: suppose our mother is ill, perhaps she has Alzheimer's. In that day and age, we would have gone to our local practitioner and discussed with him what should happen, and there probably would have been a state home for the elderly. Our mother would probably have been admitted there, and the state would probably have taken responsibility for looking after her. We would have basically handed the care of our mother over to this state agency, and they would have looked after her.

Nowadays what's likely to happen? You go to your local practitioner, and then a range of other organizations get involved, not just one. Perhaps your mother wants to stay at home, which is now plausible (apart from anything else, it's probably a bit cheaper) but she can't do much for herself. Maybe she needs help in the daytime, so one organization will provide care. Then if something goes wrong, she has to go to the hospital, so the hospital is also involved in her care. Perhaps she can't manage to cook for herself anymore, so there's probably another organization that's responsible for bringing food at lunchtime and in the evening. Perhaps she can't manage to walk, so there may be someone else who comes to wheel her around for a once-a-week outing. All these different organizations then get involved in delivering care.

Instead of having the one bureaucratic organization looking after your mother, what you now have is this package of organizations that form a network that collectively provides this care, and that creates an entirely new range of problems in public sector management, the most obvious one being coordination: how are you going to coordinate all of these different organizations and make sure they operate effectively alongside one another?

Questions for Discussion:

1. Have networks always existed to some extent? Are recent changes a matter of degree or of kind?

2. When might networks be detrimental?

VII. Analyzing Governance

How social science makes the world

HB: Both on the purely academic side and the applied side, recognizing that the world has changed, what should we do now? You've written many books on governance and are presumably anxious to influence the views of your colleagues with respect to the theory of governance. And then there's the question of how these ideas might apply to the little old lady who needs to get medical care, say.

Let's look at the abstract level first. You wrote a book called *A Theory of Governance*. Tell me about what motivated you to write that, and the implications of that within the academic milieu.

MB: Well, I think my most general motivation for the book was the philosophical one we discussed earlier. I wanted to undercut the idea that you could have a comprehensive scientific theory of governance. Instead, I wanted to suggest that one needs to understand the rise of the new governance—the kind of network organizations that we've been talking about—through telling an appropriate, historical story.

Instead of saying, "*It arose because of these formal circumstances—perhaps a shift from Fordism to post-Fordism, or perhaps because of the inherent rationality of markets and the inherent inefficiencies of bureaucracy*"—instead of a story along those lines, I want to say, "*The shift from bureaucracy through markets to networks was a consequence of the spread of particular sets of social science understandings. And that only happened because social scientists generated forms of knowledge that suggested that initially markets and then networks were the most efficient ways of governing the public sector.*"

At a very general level, I think what I wanted to say was—and I don't think I ever explicitly say this in the book—that we're too inclined to think of social science as something that's trying to describe and explain the world as it is. Often, a better way of thinking about social science is as something that creates the world.

I think most social scientists find the idea that social science creates the world very surprising. But if you stop and think for a minute, it's blindingly obvious, because every time an idea from the social sciences finds its way into the policymaking world and policy-makers act on it—whether Keynesian ideas about economics, or monetarist ideas about the money supply, or network ideas about network governance—whichever it is, once the idea makes its way from the social scientific community into the policymaking world and then inspires a policy...

HB: It becomes real.

MB: Absolutely: it becomes real. So part of what I wanted to do was draw out the way in which social science *makes* the world. I wanted to give an account of governance that emphasized this productive aspect of social science in creating the world.

I also wanted to suggest that there was something wrong with the forms of social science that had made this world. I wanted to suggest there was something mistaken, or wrong, with those social science ideas that had promoted markets and networks as panaceas to the public sector's problems. I wanted to suggest that those forms of knowledge were rooted in the false idea that you could have organizational theories that were akin to theories in the natural sciences. I wanted to say that that's not quite right.

Though I think, for instance, that these ideas of the neoliberals and the network theorists have inspired public sector reforms, I don't think they have worked as intended, precisely because they're wrong.

The idea that the neoliberals would have told you, that introducing markets would create perfect competition, I think that's wrong. I think that what happens when you introduce markets is contingent and contestable and it depends upon the traditions in terms of which people receive and read those beliefs.

Sometimes what you actually get is gangster capitalism, as is the case, for instance, in Russia. Likewise, when people introduce networks, they rarely work as intended, because they're read and understood in different contexts.

HB: When you say these ideas are wrong, you mean wrong empirically, to the extent that they don't achieve the outcomes that they told us that they were going to achieve?

MB: When I say 'wrong', I mean *philosophically* wrong. I mean that they are premised on the mistaken idea that social science can offer accounts of the world that are equivalent to natural science. They're typically based on the idea that social science is dealing with natural kinds, as though the market was a natural phenomenon, or that networks are a natural phenomenon which can be individuated and has essences and, therefore, intrinsic properties, which I don't think is true. That's the first mistake.

The second mistake is the assumption, which follows from that first mistake, that you can offer similar types of explanations in the social sciences as in the natural sciences: that is, explanations that say, "*A formal object of a type A will produce a result B.*"

HB: A would be a causal agent of B.

MB: Yes, exactly. I think both of those are mistaken. That's what I really mean by 'wrong'.

And I think a manifestation of that wrongness is that, if you introduce policies based on this false view of natural kinds in social science, you won't get the results that are predicted.

HB: In other words, what we've then got is some form of empirical verification of this "philosophical wrongness".

MB: Something like that, yes.

Questions for Discussion:

1. Do you agree or disagree with Mark's view that, in some very real way, social science creates the world?

2. Are there serious consequences to being "philosophically wrong"?

VIII. The Mechanisms of Influence

Investigating social traction

HB: Granted that the social sciences somehow create the world in the way that you've described, it's interesting to contemplate how some ideas get picked up while others don't. What is the mechanism by which these ideas that are out there in the social-sciences either get somehow absorbed, lending themselves to the creation of the world? How does that work?

MB: Let me start with the way in which I think it would be unhelpful to address that question. I think it's unhelpful to address that question in a way that would mimic the natural sciences, by asking something like, *"What formal circumstances explain why an idea will thrive?"* If you move away from that, which is how most social scientists would want to dive into that question—they would want to say, *"Can we form a correlation between ideas?"*—once you move away from that, you're just saying, *"What, loosely, seems to be happening?"*

HB: Right, exactly.

MB: I think that the big changes in our social world are, firstly, the rise of social democracy and progressive liberalism and, therefore, of the welfare state and Keynesian policies; secondly, the rise of neoliberalism; and thirdly, I would add (but I think a lot of people wouldn't) the rise of network governance, typified in Britain by New Labour, but elsewhere by the spread of joined-up and whole-of-government arrangements.

I think, in each of those cases, the following conditions held: first, the relevant forms of knowledge, often derived from the social sciences, had been around for quite a long time. In the case of the neoliberals, people like Hayek and von Mises had been writing about the benefits of the free market and the fact that bureaucratic structures were more or less bound to fail for at least 30 or 40 years by the time neoliberalism came to power.

So, typically, there is a set of academics that have developed the ideas and started to promulgate them, quite possibly a small minority group with relatively little power in the academic world.

HB: It helps if you take over a department or two though.

MB: It can, but it's not as important as the second condition, which is that those ideas find quite a wide amount of financial backing, which helps to give them a foothold and is accompanied by things like think tanks, policy institutes, and the like. In the case of neoliberalism, we're talking about the role of things like the Adam Smith Institute: picking up these ideas, turning them into practical policies, funding academics, and transferring ideas and concepts from the academic world to the policy world.

The third one—which is kind of harder to really nail—is a sense that things are a mess and we need a solution. You could imagine having the academic ideas and even money around for a long time and no one doing anything about it. That happened with the neoliberals. It didn't happen quite so much with the rise of networks. It certainly happened with the rise of the welfare state.

So then the question is, *Why do these particular ideas get picked up?* I think what happens is that there's a sense of crisis, a sense that what's been going on isn't working. It might be that, say, World War II makes it seem unacceptable to everyone that soldiers should come back to being unemployed and homeless and not having enough to eat, or it might be that the constant rise of inflation and the appearance of litter all over the streets convinces people that something in the state is broken, which is what happened in the late 1970s.

Or it might be something that, in a sense, is a crisis that's more restricted to an intellectual and policy world, such as the view that markets aren't working and we now face a range of different problems such as failed states, which is what I think happened in the case of networks.

In all of these cases what you have is a sense of crisis and a sense that we can't carry on with the kinds of organizational structures that we're currently relying on, and we need something new.

HB: There is a sort of tipping point, as it were.

MB: Yes. At that point, I think what often happens is that it appears to people—to use one of Margaret Thatcher's phrases—as if there is no alternative. What happens then is that a set of ideas comes in and seems to offer an explanation; and the very explanation it gives points to the solution.

If you say, *"The reason why we have this urban grime, and poverty, and squalor, and why our soldiers might come back to nothing, is that we live in a world in which urbanization and the free market have gone unchecked by social values, in which we need forms of public organization to deal with these problems,"* then you're pointing towards a welfare state.

To move to the neoliberal example, if you say, *"The problem is that the public sector isn't working and it's not working because, in the public sector, there is no competition and there is no need for people to become competitive or to respond to their consumers,"* then you suggest that the solution is to introduce markets and market-like mechanisms.

To turn to a more recent example, the rise of networks, one could say, *"The problem is that markets rarely work appropriately in the public sector and they certainly don't work when you have no state institutions,"* then the solution, contained in that explanation, is to build up appropriate state institutions. Insofar as you've already ruled out bureaucratic solutions, you're left with the idea that we need networks, soft institutions, informal arrangements, relationships across the public and private sector or the public involuntary sector.

So what I think happens is that there is a sense of crisis and then a viewpoint offers a compelling narrative of why we have the problems we do, and that narrative also generates the solutions.

Questions for Discussion:

1. What is Howard referring to here by "a tipping point"?

2. To what extent do you think modern politicians deliberately create a sense of crisis to satisfy their own political agendas?

3. Who were Hayek and von Mises mentioned in this chapter and what did they believe?

IX. From Theory To Practice

Appreciating a mix of strategies

HB: Now I'd like to ask you about how all of this relates to the man or woman on the street, as I promised I would. The immediate response I could imagine somebody reading this might have is, "Well, so what? I certainly see that Professor Bevir is a knowledgeable fellow. He's got this wonderful interpretive picture of what has happened in the past and what might happen, *grosso modo*, in the future. He believes that social science needs to be philosophically recognized as fundamentally different from the natural sciences, to appreciate that in a very real sense, social science creates our world. There's this new paradigm of networks that I haven't heard of before. Twenty years ago it was a different paradigm, and twenty years from now it will likely be yet another paradigm. But what does that mean for me? How can I react and respond to what you're telling me in some coherent way? How does it lead towards me living in a world with better governance, more responsive governance?"

You recently wrote a book on a new theory of governance. You wrote the OUP book *Governance: A Very Short Introduction*. You're a governance guy. So tell me how a non-political person on the street in Wichita, Birmingham or Calcutta, can further the cause of better governance for herself and her fellow citizens.

That's a hard question, and I appreciate that it's not really your job, but I'm sitting next to you so I thought I'd ask.

MB: It is hard. And it's also hard because I don't know which of several angles to come at it from. One angle would be the issues that are raised by governance.

Once you see that we live in a world where there are still the legacies of bureaucracy (as I said earlier, I think that's still the primary way in which government is organized, although we definitely have greater contracting out and the spread of markets) then you have this complex world where each of these different organizations, or forms of organization, creates a different way of linking the state to civil society.

If you imagine that you've got a bureaucracy, what you've really got is a form of command and control whereby the state will say what will go on—and, loosely speaking, that's what then goes on.

When you have a market, what you're relying on is that you have a price mechanism working alongside competition, rather than command and control.

In a network, what you have is something like trust and negotiation. Each of those models of organization might be appropriate to different sorts of activities.

For instance, if we face a strong internal terrorist threat, or if, say, our house is on fire, we probably want something that looks a bit like command and control.

Imagine if it were a market and you had to ring up five different fire stations and find out the different prices they would charge to put out the fire and decide which one you want to pay to come and put out your fire. Or imagine it being a network, where everyone would be sitting around discussing how best to be maximally coordinated and maximally efficient in order to begin to put out the fire.

So there are some circumstances where something like command and control looks really good.

Then there are other circumstances where markets might look really good. We might feel that we don't have many social values that are at stake. It's not about people's rights. We don't feel that there's a need for immediate control and authority. Maybe the market will help to drive prices down. That's a good thing.

In other areas, a network might look great. Imagine that we're talking about international aid. The idea that the USAID just tells Liberia what it's going to do in Liberia seems silly. What you want is the US working alongside non-governmental organizations like Oxfam, coordinating their activity, and also working with the Liberian government, Liberian local authorities, and Liberian NGOs.

So it seems, *prima facie*, that each of these different types of organizations is suited to different tasks. I think that one aspect of the complexity of governance is that it gets us as citizens to think about what organization we want governments to have as they interact with civil society in different activities. And I don't think there's one right or uniform answer.

Some societies might want their old people looked after by the state, other societies might want their old people to be looked after through networks of organizations. Different sets of values are at play, and we, as a society, should debate what we want to happen in different circumstances.

That's one very important thing. We should think more deeply and profoundly than we do about the kinds of values and structures we have and move beyond the standard newspaper binary of market vs. hierarchy, itself seen as an "all or nothing" ideological construct, and instead think about what kinds of relationships we want in what sorts of circumstances.

So that would be one very general answer to your question.

Another would be that I think that recognizing the network nature of governance draws attention to a range of problems that the public sector, in particular, faces today that otherwise would be missed. Particularly if you're a policymaker or a public sector worker, I think it can help you to better manage your tasks.

For instance, if you see that we have this mix of strategies, then you will see the importance of the role of managing these strategies for government and for public-sector workers, managing the mix between markets, networks, and hierarchies. That's a very complex thing.

If, for instance, you create a network with the idea that it is going to govern things, then you lose a degree of control. If then, as a public sector manager, you try to come back and exert that control, then you're reasserting hierarchy over the network. You have a trade-off, and you need to think through which of those trade-offs you want.

Once you accept, say, that what you want is a network, or your higher-ups tell you that you will operate a network, then you have to think about how to manage that network as best you can, or how to manage this market as best you can. These ideas can guide the ways we think about these things.

Finally, I think that the extent to which my theory challenges reified concepts and models of social science that ape natural science means that my theory suggests we should stop thinking about these problems—our relationship to civil society and the way public managers deal with their domain—in terms of social science giving us solutions, and instead we should think in more participatory and dialogic modes.

Which is all to say that my general response to the question, *How do we manage the mix of markets, networks, and hierarchies?* is simply that we should promote dialogue and participation.

Question for Discussion:

1. What role does the media play in communicating scholarly ideas in the social sciences? Are they doing a good job? If not, how might they be improved?

X. Doing Things Better

The importance of listening

HB: This is all of a piece, it seems to me, with the question of how best to create a society. Presumably the more dialogue we have, the more views will come into play and the greater likelihood that we all can have a real impact on what actually comes to pass. Which all sounds wonderful, but I don't say this without a certain amount of scepticism.

You mentioned the word 'utopian' before in a different context. Here's my scepticism. As you've pointed out, developing meaningful dialogue requires judgment and sensitivity, because you can't rely on pat solutions, or pat stereotypes, or simplistic "market good, state bad" dichotomies (or the other way around), or any of this silliness. You have to be able to be sufficiently intellectually dexterous and intellectually honest to move on a case-by-case basis, between different possibilities so as to not only say, *"This is the case when my house is on fire, so it calls for this particular solution as opposed to that particular solution",* but you also have to look at the subtleties of, examining, say, if you decide networks are the best solution, then what sorts of networks, and how best do we move forwards?

I see that as being logically possible, but on a practical level I'm somewhat sceptical that we, as a society, can get our act together to get people involved at a high enough dialogical level. My principle source of scepticism—I keep coming back to this—actually lies with the media. After all, if we can't even get that story straight that you were telling me before—that we've moved ahead beyond 20-year-old, outdated dichotomies that the media are still portraying to people— and if we can't adequately respond to what people like yourself, and what policymakers, firmly believe, then that leads me to conclude that we have a lot of work to do before we reach this happy day when citizens can engage and start participating in that dialogue.

MB: Well, on the one hand, I think that's what we already do. We already live in a world that's messy and where people are constantly making little judgments. I think we already do the things you're saying are complex. Therefore, the question is whether or not we can learn to do them better, not whether we can do them at all.

Once you rephrase the question, something similar could still arise. You could still say, *"Is the way to do them better really to give everyday citizens a much greater role in terms of participation in dialogue?"* That, I think, is a real problem, at least in some cases. I think there is always a trade-off between believing that people should participate and decide for themselves, and believing that you know what they should decide. You have to choose whether you're going to privilege the process of them deciding or your view of what's right. And that occurs everywhere.

Think of the role of, say, a Bill of Rights in a constitution. What these really say is, *The people can decide what they want democratically, but they can't decide to go **against** these rights.*

We're always going to have things that we're particularly reluctant to let people override through making their own decisions, and we're always going to have a space where we want people to make those decisions. The question is, how do we navigate that?

What I'm about to say is going to sound like a more reactionary statement than I would like it to, so I should preface it by saying that I do think participation is good and that people should actively seek to promote participation. But when I talk about participation and dialogue I don't necessarily mean processes of radical participatory decision-making in which the majority decides the issue, or even in which decisions are made by arriving at some sort of consensus.

If you imagine a deeply divided community—Northern Ireland, or Israel perhaps—you can imagine the majority willingly passing a range of policies that would be unacceptable in terms of what they did to the minority.

You can imagine, in policy terms, group A saying, *"In order to qualify for public housing, you must be a member of group A,"* and because group A is a majority, that policy goes through. That's clearly unacceptable irrespective of whether we have a right to public housing in a Bill of Rights or not. That level of unequal treatment is unacceptable.

HB: And that can happen within a completely democratic framework.

MB: Exactly. So I think there are good reasons to not take what I'm saying to straightforwardly mean majority decision-making. What I am insisting that is virtually always good is that policymakers— irrespective of whether they rely on majority decision-making and radical participatory procedures for decision-making—should involve the citizens in a dialogical process.

The reason I think that is virtually always good is because, if you are convinced that social science can predict in a law-like way how your citizens are going to behave when you introduce a policy, then you will be convinced ahead of time what the consequences of that policy are going to be.

But once you reject the idea that social science can tell you that a population is bound to react in a certain way, then you come to think that the way in which the population is going to react is necessarily contingent; it depends on the existing beliefs and desires of the population, which are typically somewhat consistent but may also change slightly through the process.

In those circumstances, I think policymakers will almost always do well to involve the public—the targets of their policy—in a dialogic process, if only to learn more about how the policy is likely to work out. Even if, after listening to the target group of the policy, they ended up deciding that they definitely do not want to do what the majority want—even if that's the case, I think the policy will be improved and will be more likely to have the eventual outcomes wished for if they have been through a dialogic process. The policymakers will be more sensitive to the beliefs and desires of those they think the policy will influence, and, therefore better able to craft and fine-tune the policy so that it fits those beliefs and desires.

Questions for Discussion:

1. Are there better and worse ways to have a dialogue between policymakers and citizens? Discuss.

2. How might the threat of a tyranny of the majority be best dealt with in a modern liberal democracy?

XI. Starting Over

A lone wolf takes charge, at least theoretically

HB: This is all very comprehensible, logical, and reasonable, it seems to me. But, moving to the über-practical, if you will—say you've just been elected President of the United States or, perhaps better still, you're the Prime Minister of the United Kingdom with a majority government, which means that you can effectively do whatever you want. What would you do?

Perhaps that's too broad a question, so let me pose another instead. How might you change the way governance is carried out writ large? What might you do at the meta-level with respect to governance, were you in a position to make such a change?

MB: I have to reinterpret your question a bit, because I think that one's attitude to tolerance means that you can agree that something should be allowed to happen without approving of it. For instance, if I could dictate what goes on in this department, I wouldn't want to force everyone to do the kind of social science I favour, because I believe that there should be other strategies. Nonetheless, I naturally favour my type of social science.

Analogously, were I Prime Minister, what I would want is to allow other people to do what they want, in some sense.

But if you ask me what might best suit me, I think I would want to wipe out social science as we currently know it. That's a very strong claim, I know. But if I am right in my diagnosis, then many of the root problems of contemporary social life come from thinking that social science is a natural science, and therefore relying on formal explanations that either reify social concepts like class, bureaucracy, or network, or reify human rationality so that you can offer formal models of it.

This act of reification then inspires formal explanations so that they seem to ape the natural sciences and are divorced from historically contingent intentionality. If I'm right in my diagnosis, then that's the source of a lot of our problems. It means that people constantly think that social science will provide solutions, and it doesn't. Which, in turn, means that we're constantly ruled by people saying, *"Here's the solution."*

And it's not just government. Whichever organization you're in, you will have been subjected to markets and networks as modes of governance. You will find that the way in which you are employed has changed. Perhaps you now have to do more contract work rather than being employed within an organization. Perhaps your standing of employment is less secure. Perhaps the organization you work in is flatter. Perhaps now you're meant to spend more of your time building network relationships with other similar organizations rather than managing people under you.

You can see the same thing when you look at how our health is now governed in hospitals. In Britain, for instance, you have the general practitioners who will now purchase hospital treatment from different hospitals.

Our whole life—where we're employed, how our health is managed, how we're educated—all these organizations are increasingly governed by ideas coming from the social sciences, which, as I see it, are premised on this error: they're premised on reification followed by formal explanation.

What I would like to see is the replacement of those forms of knowledge by more humanistic forms of knowledge: that is, forms of knowledge that recognize that people are intentional agents who act for conscious, subconscious, and unconscious reasons of their own, where those reasons are products of their wider webs of belief, which are things that they loosely inherit from historical traditions.

Once you make that shift in the form of knowing, I don't know what will happen. I can't say, *"To change the form of knowledge will be to generate this or that."* Of course, if I could say something like that—

HB: You'd be part of the problem.

MB: Exactly. I'd be contradicting myself: offering a formal account of what will necessarily arise.

Sometimes when I'm faced with critics, I analogize what I'm saying to one plausible reading of Marx and his view of communism, which is that he knows he doesn't like capitalism; he thinks there should be a revolution, but he can't anticipate what communism would look like. It's only later, once you get the rise of what I'm thinking of as modern social science that communists start to say, *"The answer to that question is collective ownership of the means of production by which we mean state ownership and state planning."* It was inconceivable for Marx himself to think in those terms. Those categories weren't around in the 19th century.

There's this more open-ended way of thinking of things where what you want to do is get rid of what's there and—precisely because what you want to promote in its place is something like a greater and more humanistic perspective more rooted in people's freedom, meaningful choice, and collective action, together in pursuit of what they think is human flourishing—you can't tell them what they should then be doing.

HB: Is this perspective catching on, you think, or are you a lone wolf in this regard?

MB: I think I'm probably, if not a lone wolf, at least one of a very small pack.

HB: OK. But is the pack gaining some form of momentum, at least?

MB: I'm not sure about that. I think it's gaining momentum insofar as I am increasingly aware of academic organizations that bring together people who think things a bit like this, such as people who favour interpretive approaches to social science. But that could just be that, as I work more and more on this, I get invited to speak to more and more of these sorts of organizations. So it might be that we are a growing minority, or it might just be that I am more aware of the groups and organizations that are sympathetic to this perspective, and those have always been there.

Questions for Discussion:

1. How have specific aspects of your life been affected by recent trends in the social sciences?

2. Do you think that Mark's views will get greater (lesser?) currency in the academic world as time goes on?

XII. Going Global

Encouraging pluralism and open patterns

HB: Is there anything that one can abstract away from this conversation that might apply more particularly to global governance, pan-national governance, the United Nations, or what have you? You mentioned NGOs before when we were talking about networks. Is there anything that one can say within the spirit of what we've been talking about that leads to some particular insight on a different scale, on a meta-national level?

MB: I think many of the same issues would arise. At a very general level, for instance, I think there was a time—think of when the League of Nations was created, or, to some extent, even the UN itself—when the only conceivable alternatives for world order were either something that looked like an anarchy of states or global government, where you had formal hierarchical institutions like the League of Nations or the United Nations.

One moral that comes across from the literature on governance is that even order within states is much messier than that: it's never straightforwardly hierarchical, but that doesn't mean you have anarchy. This opens us up to seeing global governance as something that is itself a mess—not necessarily in a bad way, but a mess that arises out of a mix of some hierarchical institutions, which would include the UN, but would also perhaps include regional organizations like the EU. It would also include networks—perhaps, say, a network of organizations that will go in and try and deal with the aftermath of the earthquake in Japan, or the aftermath of the Haiti disaster. It would also include market relationships, perhaps within trading blocs, or perhaps more globally. All of these things are, in fact, parts of global government; and they are all governed, more or less formally or informally, by human agents.

So one thing this does, I think, is open us up to a more nuanced picture of what we might mean by global governance. Once you do that, then you open some of the same theoretical questions. You open up the question of what we want the relationship to be between government and civil society.

In the case of global governance, that's made slightly more complex because now what you're saying is, *"What do we want the relationship to be between global organizations, states, and civil society?"* I personally often favour something like global civil society, and I'm often quite hostile to states. But I think global civil society should interact with international organizations.

So I think we face the same moral questions about what sorts of levels we want to be governed by here. To continue that idea, I think we face something like the same question about imposition—whether we're willing to impose things on people—just as we saw when we looked at the notion that having a Bill of Rights restricts what goes on, but in certain cases people are free to make their choices.

What do we want to say to whole clusters of people, the vast majority of whom want to do something differently? What do we say if there's a society, the vast majority of which really don't want democracy and instead just want a stable government that will hopefully help the economy to grow? What do we say to a society that systematically—including the women themselves—thinks women should not be as well educated as men? What right do we necessarily have to try to impose our beliefs?

I think we often might have a right, but we need to be careful to wonder what it is.

And if we do think we have a right, is it one that's best exercised through some sort of global hierarchy, or is it one that should really be done through networks, including, ideally, networks that involve dissident members of the society we're trying to transform?

HB: As you were talking, I was thinking that, typically, the view is that world government is this quasi-utopian idea, and for all practical purposes we have to wait until we get our individual national governments sorted out and make sure they're actually functional before we start taking the question of world government at all seriously.

But according to what you were saying, things might actually work the other way around. One could imagine creating a more tolerant, effective, narrative-based elimination of formal social science systems that is applied, as a general ethos, in a global scenario, with all of its messy, complicated players. Then, if that starts to bear fruit in some objective way, it might actually 'trickle down', as it were, towards national governments. Is that conceivable, you think?

MB: I think so. I certainly think the following is true: I think that the absence of a global government, the absence of something that looks like the federal government of the United States ruling over the whole globe, say, means it's easier to appreciate and navigate your way around a messy patchwork of governing organizations that involve a greater role being given to markets, networks—and particularly in my case, to civil society organizations—and to see that as acceptable, rather than as a failure of government in the way that one would within a state.

I also think that, in terms of the global order, the fact that we are obviously dealing with a world of states means that we more dramatically confront the question of multiculturalism. We confront fairly dramatically the question, *"What right have we got to make them do what we think best if they disagree?"* If not always, I think, at least at times, we are going to be more pluralistic in our attitude to other states than we would be to other groups within our own society. We're going to extend a greater range of rights to them.

Often, within the United States for instance, 'multiculturalism' really just means, *Tolerate different groups, but only tolerate them to the extent that they, too, are tolerating other groups*. We're not really assigning distinct rights to them to engage in practices that we think are harmful and wrong. Whereas when we're dealing with states, we might naturally be more willing to do that.

I think, then, that there is something about the global order that facilitates the rise of more pluralistic and open patterns of social organization—for both better and worse, it should be said.

The better is that it's more pluralistic and open and people can do what they want; the worse is that you're less able to effectively rule out the things you really don't like.

HB: Thanks very much, Mark. This has been a fascinating conversation. Is there anything we've omitted that you'd like to add?

MB: No, we covered a lot.

HB: Well, that was great, thanks.

MB: My pleasure.

Questions for Discussion:

1. *What role might philanthropy play in the development of a more progressive global society?*

2. *Does the notion of "global civil society" itself imply a level of shared values? If so, which ones?*

Continuing the Conversation

Readers are encouraged to read Mark's books, *Governance: A Very Short Introduction* and *A Theory of Governance*, which formed the basis of this conversation and go into considerable additional detail about many of the issues discussed here.

Exploring Southeast Asia

A conversation with Jacques Bertrand

Introduction

A Prescription for Progress

In many ways political science has always irritated me.

First off, there is the issue of its very name, which is clearly a hubristic sort of misnomer—there is nothing remotely scientific about "political science", and any attempt to genuinely pretend otherwise will quickly land one into all sorts of trouble, invoking notions of "laws" and "experiments" where none, in reality, exist.

Then there is the fact that so many political scientists seem determined to slip into punditry positions, cheerfully sticking their faces into the camera to trivialize complex geopolitical situations as they not so subtly pump sales of their invariably sensationalist and inflammatory popular books.

The astute observer might point out that none of this is particularly unique to political science. In fact, a quick perusal at the popular science section of any bookstore will be enough to convince any critical thinker that the "real" sciences are also littered with people desperately trying to promote their own sensationalistic popular interpretations of things, often in a decidedly underwhelmingly non-scientific way. Indeed, it's tempting to conclude that the only reason you generally don't find *these* people also sticking their faces into the cameras of popular news shows to talk about their pet theories of the universe is that nobody has bothered to do so.

Which brings up a central point: the reason why most average people have at some point encountered the smug assertions of those declaring "*The Clash of Civilizations*" or "*The End of History*" while generally remaining removed from the dogmatic sputterings of inflationary cosmologists, say, is precisely because political science, by its very nature and orientation, is vastly more relevant and impactful to people than many other disciplines.

As Cambridge University political theorist John Dunn once exasperatedly expressed it:

> "The fact is people **do** need political comprehension; and the way in which political science has been institutionalized over time is hugely unhelpful—most of it doesn't provide much political comprehension."

Those words were ringing in my ears as I spoke with University of Toronto political scientist Jacques Bertrand, who strikes me as precisely the sort of thoughtful, responsible political scientist who can help us. His intriguingly synoptic book, *Political Change in Southeast Asia*, contains no pat thesis or sweeping call to action, but instead carefully and methodically describes the remarkable historical, cultural, religious, political and economic diversity throughout a region that many of us—myself most definitely included—know alarmingly little about.

Indeed, if there is one clear generalization that one can make about this part of the world it is that it's remarkably, distinctively, diverse—a fact that naturally presents its own inherent challenges to specialists.

> "Most specialists of Africa or Latin America will usually know at least three or four countries in their region pretty well. They might be embarrassed that they don't know the other thirty as well, but, when you study Africa there are certain trends or themes that will come up, such as the colonial history. Whether it was the English or the French, there's a commonality in the forms of colonialism that occurred in Africa that make scholars look at it and see certain trends in poverty, inequality, marginalization and so forth that they can trace back to a particular historical backdrop of colonialism and how it evolved.

> "But when you confront Southeast Asia, you'll find some countries that come out of fairly consolidated attempts at building empires, other areas where there was practically no political consolidation

before European colonizers came, and anything in between. There were many changes in borders, and some cultures where borders didn't even matter: it was the control of people that mattered not the borders, so you're often not exactly sure where to demarcate beginning and end in terms of expressions of territorial meaning. Typically, the meaning of "states" and "territory" really comes much later; and in some ways it's the history of European colonialism that establishes the idea of "states with borders" in the region.

"So when we study Southeast Asia, the idea of knowing the region really well is oftentimes limited: many people who study Southeast Asia will really only know one country, and maybe a second. And this means that once people start making claims about several countries we start to get a little nervous, because you almost never know three or four Southeast Asian languages, so the depth that you can capture by going from one country to the next is quickly lost when you can't communicate anymore in the local language."

And suddenly, the question gets turned on its head. Rather than looking at political science through the simplifying lens of grand-standing pundits, the question becomes, *How, in light of such striking diversity, can we make sense of **anything** at all?* If every example has its accompanying counterexample, if every trend has its exceptions, to what extent are we able to say anything more than merely, *"It's complicated"*—particularly about a place that we don't have any shared personal experience with?

According to Jacques, the answer lies in a methodical, case-by-case application of a combination of what he calls "factors of explanation"—carefully invoking established concepts such as democracy, conflict, economic liberalization, and social progress—***together with*** a deep understanding of historical circumstances.

"We're not going to have a theoretical proposition that holds under all circumstances—at some level the social world just doesn't work like that. But when we're trying to study political phenomena and political change, we have to have a vocabulary, we have to have something that we can compare. Meanwhile, although I'm

*sympathetic to history and sympathetic to cultural differences, what I resist is the idea that we're simply telling a **story**, because that's what happens in the end if you emphasize too much diversity."*

Such sober calls for caution and speculative restraint will likely not result in bestselling popular books, but they are, I'm convinced, a necessary part of actually understanding what's going on around us.

The Conversation

I. Plunging In

Indonesian immersion

HB: How did you get involved in Southeast Asia? What's the story there?

JB: I wish there was a fascinating story to tell there but it was mostly a standard story of progressing in the academic world, actually—a lot of people get into a region such as Southeast Asia because they went on some very impactful exchange program or something when they were younger, but that wasn't my experience.

Interestingly, many people don't even ask that question if it's a region that's more well-known, whereas with Southeast Asia one usually asks; but I don't have a particularly special story to tell except that I was an international relations student looking at broad issues across the world—when you're dealing with that broad perspective you don't get to know the issues on the ground and any real detail—and I didn't have an obvious region that I had certain affinities to.

But I did know what I had an interest in: I was particularly interested in Indonesia, which struck me as a unique country as well as an extremely challenging one given that it's an archipelago with lots of different languages and peoples and so forth. Perhaps it was a result of growing up in Canada, regularly encountering diversity and different languages and issues around these languages, that a place like Indonesia, with so many different languages and peoples yet held together as a country, was so fascinating and intriguing to me. So, perhaps that's what started me going to Indonesia, and that region in general.

HB: And when was this? What stage of your education were you at when you first went to Indonesia?

JB: I was a PhD student. In the first year of my PhD I was already thinking about China, Indonesia and so forth—these were countries that I was getting interested in—so I rapidly thought that I needed to get to know an entire region better.

As I just mentioned, I found that dealing with only broad, international issues didn't get me to understand the intricacies of what was really going on in particular countries very well. I was writing papers on issues on economic development—I did some Master's work on international, political economy—and it was odd for me to be writing and thinking about economic development without actually seeing on the ground what it truly means to understand how the state is trying to develop certain areas or is trying to inject certain incentives to produce more in agriculture or manufacturing or in any other areas of development.

So, I took a little bit of a break and embarked on a very different tangent at that point—and, in fact, in some ways, I probably overreacted and went from a PhD student doing international relations to a PhD student who ended up writing a dissertation about village politics in Indonesia.

HB: I'd like to probe you on this a little more because some of this I think I understand, but other parts I don't. I see that you're at Princeton and wondering to yourself how you're going to be able to say anything truly meaningful and relevant about all this general stuff like international relations and large-scale economic trends without a genuine understanding of what life is like on the ground for the people concerned. That part I get.

But then how, specifically, you wind up in a particular Indonesian village is somewhat mystifying to me. Did you just take a dart and throw it at a map and wind up in a certain place in Indonesia? Did you go on a backpacking trip and have particular formative experiences? How did that actually come about?

JB: I actually went to China before my PhD. China was a country that I found fascinating for many obvious reasons. I went to minority regions in China on a backpacking trip, so I was already interested in travelling in Asia and understanding Asia, so China was my first foray into the region actually.

Meanwhile, I had friends who had been to Indonesia, so first learning through friends and then reading more background in detail, I came to understand how that country was different from others and found myself increasingly attracted to the region.

I had actually started to learn the language as well at that point. When I first went to Indonesia, I was actually going on an advanced language course: I had taken a year in my PhD studies to go to Cornell and do an intensive language training course because Princeton did not have an intensive language course in Indonesian.

Cornell was a known center for Southeast Asian studies and had an in-depth language studies program associated with it—this intensive language program—and Indonesian was a language that was fairly accessible, one that someone could learn fairly rapidly compared to, say, Mandarin,—which, if you're a late starter, can be a very difficult endeavour for several years.

Unlike Mandarin, Indonesian is phonetic—you don't have characters, you don't have to learn the written language separately from the spoken language—so, it was an interesting adventure to say, *"Okay, I'm going to learn this for a year and then I'll start looking into working in Indonesia"*, simply because I was interested in the country—never thinking that I would necessarily become a specialist and stay on for that many years. But it ended up working out that way.

HB: So, I'd like to get to the "many years" bit shortly, but just back to the language for a moment: I'm ashamed to say I know nothing about this language although I think, in your book, there was some Indonesian word related to the language—I think it begins with a "B"...

JB: Yes: "Bahasa Indonesia". "Bahasa" simply means language in Malay. Sometimes in English, people wrongly refer to it as just "bahasa"—which doesn't actually mean anything more than "language"—so the Indonesian language is "bahasa Indonesia".

The reality of this language is that it's a dialect of Malay. Malay was the lingua franca of the Southeast Asian archipelago excluding the Philippines.

Indonesia was created as a country out of a nationalist movement that decided, quite consciously to take the Malay that was being spoken across the islands as a unifying symbol, if you like, of what made them one people—so that dialect of Malay was renamed as the Indonesian Language.

HB: So, it is a dialect? When you go to Malaysia, can you understand what people are saying there?

JB: I can understand a good part of what is spoken there, yes.

HB: You mentioned its phonetic nature. What's the alphabet?

JB: It's the Roman alphabet. At some point they used Arabic script to write it but they changed it to the Roman alphabet, so once you know how to pronounce Indonesian, you can read it.

It's a relatively easy language to learn in that respect—or, at least, a satisfying language to learn in the beginning because you learn rapidly, and then it gets more difficult when it gets to more elaborate ways of conveying meaning.

HB: Interesting. OK, so you went to Cornell for this intense language course...

JB: Yes: eight months or so of courses and then the last three months were in Indonesia, living with a family associated with a local university, being immersed in that environment.

In fact, this was very interesting because this was in Java, and so many other students were placed in families where oftentimes the language of communication was Javanese. So, many of the other students didn't benefit as much from their immersion experience because they were hearing Javanese and not Indonesian.

In my case, however, I was placed with a faculty member who was actually alone and had a lot of students from different parts of the archipelago living at his place and doing Masters degrees, so it was a very nice community to learn about different areas of the archipelago and also to learn the language because Indonesian was constantly spoken around the house.

It worked out particularly well for me because some of those Masters students—at the time Masters students were sometimes faculty in their own universities in outer islands—became very helpful contacts for me when I ended up doing some of my PhD research in a completely other part of Indonesia.

HB: So, through this process you developed the opportunity to further explore the country in a far deeper way than you would have otherwise had access to.

JB: That's right—and it directly exposed me to the issues that were arising in different parts of Indonesia related to issues such as diversity. If they were from Maluku, for example, I would hear expressions of their resentment towards what, at the time, was the military government of President Suharto.

And don't forget that this was occurring in the middle of Java—the principal region of Indonesia representing the majority of the country's population—so the kinds of issues that would sometimes come up around the table had to do with the resentment of over-centralization of the government but also the impact of the Javanese in government.

HB: So you could get your hands dirty very quickly.

JB: Exactly. So, I knew at that point that this was what I wanted to do because it just kept getting more and more fascinating to me. I had taken a bit of a risk by learning another language for eight months, but it turned out to be well worth it because it quickly became clear to me that Indonesia was a place I wanted to study; and the more I travelled, the more I found the country beautiful as well: it was very interesting to explore.

HB: I'd like to broaden a bit from Indonesia, but something you said intrigued me just now when you were talking about the language and you mentioned the difference between Javanese and Indonesian. How different are they?

JB: They are quite different. Javanese vocabulary is completely different, I couldn't understand Javanese. Javanese also has different levels of language, which doesn't exist in Indonesian: so you'll learn three different kinds of languages in order to be able to speak to, for instance, an elderly person or the Sultan or something, while if you're speaking to somebody younger, you'd often use a different registry of language.

Questions for Discussion:

1. *What does the fact that people are more inclined to ask how somebody became a Southeast Asian scholar than a "more well-known region" reveal about our own cultural biases?*

2. *Are there academic advantages to opting to focus on "less established" or "less popular" subject areas? To what extent are some scholars more inclined to go "off the beaten track" than others?*

II. Recognizing Complexity

Appreciating individual trajectories

HB: I don't know if this was a strongly influencing factor for you—from what you've told me, it seems like your career trajectory was quite organic and natural—but for me, as a non-specialist, I was struck by the fact that this part of the world contains a really striking amount of diversity in a relatively contained, geographical region.

Not only are there so many different languages, religions, political systems and so forth, there are also so many different historical trajectories, from colonial experiences under the Dutch, British and French, say, as well as regions that managed to effectively combat colonialism and remain independent.

Then, of course, you have the effects of the Cold War, with some on one side and some on another, and then its aftermath.

So, it seems to be a fascinating microcosm of studying all sorts of different factors simultaneously that I could imagine would make for remarkably fertile ground for an international relations specialist.

Were you thinking about this yourself as you became more and more involved in living in the region and exploring it? Were you particularly conscious of its relevance as a "test case" for all of these different factors and variety, or were you more pulled in by the particular appeal of your environment and your personal experiences?

JB: As you say, the region is very diverse, and as a scholar this presents advantages and challenges. In studying a region as diverse as Southeast Asia, you quickly bump into many linguistic differences, cultural differences and so forth.

So, to answer your question: when I began to study the region, I was certainly struck by its diversity, which I found very interesting, but also somewhat intimidating as well.

Southeast Asianists—

HB: That's a real term?

JB: It's a real term, yes, and one with its own particular challenges, compared to, say, Africanists or Latin Americanists, to denote specialists of their regions.

Most specialists of Africa or Latin America will usually know at least three or four countries in their region pretty well. They might be embarrassed that they don't know the other thirty as well, but, when you study Africa there are certain trends or themes that will come up, such as the colonial history. Whether it was the English or the French, there's a commonality in the forms of colonialism that occurred in Africa that make scholars look at it and see certain trends in poverty, inequality, marginalization and so forth that they can trace back to a particular historical backdrop of colonialism and how it evolved.

But when you confront Southeast Asia, you'll find some countries that come out of fairly consolidated attempts at building empires, other areas where there was practically no political consolidation before European colonizers came, and anything in between. There were many changes in borders, and some cultures where borders didn't even matter: it was the control of people that mattered not the borders, so you're often not exactly sure where to demarcate beginning and end in terms of expressions of territorial meaning. Typically, the meaning of "states" and "territory" really come much later; and in some ways it's the history of European colonialism that establishes the idea of "states with borders" in the region.

So when we study Southeast Asia, the idea of knowing the region really well is oftentimes limited: many people who study Southeast Asia will really only know one country, and maybe a second. And this means that once people start making claims about several countries we start to get a little nervous, because you almost never know three or four Southeast Asian languages, so the depth that you can capture by going from one country to the next is quickly lost when you can't communicate anymore in the local language.

HB: That reminds me of what I saw in some of the blurbs on the back of your book, *Political Change in Southeast Asia*. Of course blurbs on books often have to be taken with a grain or two of salt, but I was struck by the fact that they were all of the form, *"Finally, somebody has written a sweeping, comparative account of all these different countries in Southeast Asia. It's remarkable what this guy's done because he's able to compare and contrast and examine political, economic, historical and cultural trends in more than one country at a time."*

And I was particularly struck by that, because as an outsider I was thinking, *What's the big deal here? Isn't that the typical sort of thing that a scholar in this area would be producing?*

But this actually ties in to what you were just saying—it's quite unusual to even attempt to make such broad, sweeping comparisons amongst Southeast Asian countries due to the region's extraordinary diversity.

JB: The blurbs are flattering, I have to say. As you correctly noted, the blurbs might be sometimes a little exaggerated but they do convey what I was trying to say which is that there are few who have attempted to look at Southeast Asia in such a broad, comparative way.

It's one thing to compare lots of countries, this is standard practice in political science. But when you're looking at "factors of explanation" and examining certain trends in many different countries—perhaps you're thinking about "democracy" or "conflict"—you always place yourself at a certain "coarse-grained" level of analysis that enables you to do that, but which is naturally also a limitation.

Once you start delving into differences and detail, it quickly becomes impossible to such a broad-brush comparison at that level, but it's still feasible to do in some regions: you can still develop both a regional and in-depth look at certain countries when, historically, culturally or economically there are many clear parallels.

What is so challenging for anybody trying to make comparisons in Southeast Asia is that the more you deepen your understanding of countries, the more their differences become clear.

Which means that if you want to be able to say something meaningful about what's similar, what's different, and *why*, it's often quite a challenge because the contrasts become so large.

So what I tried to do—and hopefully I did it in a reasonably successful way—is to do a little bit of both: invoking both a regional and in-depth perspective.

I tried to look at the region and think about why the region looks the way it does politically. Why are some countries democratic? Why are some authoritarian? Why have some seen such rapid change to the point that people began talking about, the new "tigers" of Asia—those that were clearly rapidly developing and having very high growth rates—while others were lagging behind, and so forth.

But I also tried to understand a little more in-depth why it was that, say, Indonesia, with its particular history, can manage to develop economically, whereas a place like Cambodia ended up in war and destruction and all sorts of division.

HB: Right. I'd like to get into one of the primary regional groupings that you make—because, as you imply, however rough and ready such categorizations are, you clearly have to impose some sort of order structure to examine things or you can't get started, fully aware that every time you try to do anything, you run the risk of perhaps oversimplifying things and placing countries and sub-regions in the wrong box.

But before I ask you about that, I have a very specific question. My sense is that you treated the whole region, but you left out Brunei. Do you have something against Brunei?

JB: Uh, no. I have nothing against Brunei. There were various limitations imposed by a publisher who tells you the length the book has to be, and in the end, it came down to me having to grapple with the question of what I could possibly get away with leaving out. So I eventually settled on Brunei because it was the tiniest country with not a whole lot to explain, relatively speaking, in terms of change, and there was already a lot that I was trying to pack into the book.

HB: Fair enough. I wasn't actually being serious, by the way—merely pointing out, in my own facetious way, the enormous breadth of your project.

Anyway, let me return to this issue of your principal categorization procedure. My sense is that the main distinction, structurally, that you make is between what you call capitalist countries and state socialism and authoritarian stability.

This seems to be the legacy of the Cold war: that you have the countries that were a part of the communist world—namely Vietnam, Laos, Cambodia and Myanmar—which can be contrasted with Indonesia, Thailand, Malaysia, the Philippines, East Timor and Singapore.

Is that a pretty standard and well-accepted way of grouping countries in the region, or did you have some push back from people who disagreed with that particular categorization procedure?

JB: In the field, I think there would be a common understanding that the state-socialist countries had a very different experience than the other capitalist, market-oriented economies. It's also a reasonable way of grouping countries politically throughout the region, because the original ASEAN—the Association of Southeast Asian Nations—only consisted of non-communist states.

So I think most scholars would not quibble with that distinction. A related question, however, is the relative impact of the Cold War on the region. Personally, I found that many scholars who concentrated on regional differences put too great an emphasis on the role of the Cold War.

Clearly the Cold War was a determining period of history that influenced the direction of many different countries in Southeast Asia and elsewhere. And obviously one of the reasons why Southeast Asia became a very strong region of study in the 1970s was the Vietnam War: there was a great deal of interest in trying to understand what was happening in Vietnam and the effects of the Vietnam War, which was a principal reason why many American Universities invested a lot in trying to comprehend Southeast Asia during that period of time.

So much of the scholarly work that was done from the '70s onwards had a lot to do with the role of the United States in the region and the Vietnam War, both in itself as an extension of the Cold War.

But I like to think of it slightly different as well. I like to think of it as the history of the evolution of big ideas, and the big competing ideologies of the twentieth century.

So it was not merely at a level of realpolitik where the United States, the Soviet Union and China had their interests, it had a real impact on the flow of ideas. At a time when new states were being created and movements arose to liberate people from colonial rulers, these competing ideologies played a significant role in influencing thought, in understanding where people got their ideas from.

And that sometimes predates the Cold War by a lot. So when we go back and try to understand the origins of Vietnam or the origins of Indonesia, on the one hand there's the view of nationalism as a sort of template to create new countries as a means of self-determination, nationalism in opposition to colonial rule.

That's the nationalism that is seen as a liberating form: one that struggles against colonial rulers. And one cannot understand a country like Indonesia without understanding that it comes out of a very strong anti-colonial, nationalist movement.

In the same way, when we think about Vietnam, there is clearly this nationalist attempt to liberate themselves first from the French and then the United States, but there is also another important intellectual strand of those who were attracted to the communist ideals as a way of organizing society differently.

So when we look at the histories in the region, it shouldn't simply be regarded as a location for Cold War proxy battles between the United States and Soviet Union. That's a large part of the story, yes, but there is also the story of these movements who were searching for how they were going to express their political identities.

These were struggles, obviously, in every single country—even in countries that became strongly capitalist. At different points of time in Indonesia, in Malaysia, there were some strong, communist movements that were trying to offer a very different kind of template for how society should be structured.

Now, they eventually lost out there. The nationalists won out in Indonesia and something different emerged in Malaysia, but in Vietnam that was the important strand that eventually won out, after lots of war and division.

Questions for Discussion:

1. Under what circumstances is the historical scholarship about a region influenced by contemporary political concerns? Is there a link between "relevance" and "subjective interest"?

2. To what extent can one region, or group of regions, be objectively determined to be "more diverse" than another?

III. Authoritarianism

Another product of history

HB: So, there's the Cold War aspect to things, but there's also this issue of authoritarianism. Let me try to be very concrete and not pretend to come at things from a scholarly perspective—which is eminently appropriate because I'm very far removed from being an expert here, of course.

To the man on the street, hearing about a military junta ruling this country and a military coup occurring in that country, there might be this natural tendency to think, *The key thing to bear in mind here isn't so much which countries follow "state socialism" and which ones follow "capitalism"—the major factor is that all too often there's a military government in charge which has no real respect for the "rule of law" as we understand it.* How would you respond to that?

JB: Well, it's true: the military has been a very strong institution in many of these countries, that's the reason many of these states were actually strong states—but there's a very strong distinction between states that are "state-socialist".

And there's a reason that I use the term "state-socialist": "communist" would be a bit of a misnomer, because we associate that with the standard, communist line where you have the official communist party that has affiliations with China or the Soviet Union. But Burma was slightly different—they chose their own way. It was very much "military-first" and then an ideology of "the Burmese way to socialism". So, they took some of these ideas out of the communist template, if you like—mainly, cutting themselves off economically and having the government—and the military, by extension—own a lot of the industries.

HB: But first and foremost, predicated on a military coup.

JB: Correct. So that, in a sense, puts Burma, or Myanmar, in a funny category, because although it has this history where for more than ten or fifteen years it saw itself as "socialist", it had its own "brand" and it was certainly a military-first government.

In fact, what the Burmese military government tried to do was create a kind of communist party, "The Burmese Socialist Program Party", *after* they were in power, and use what has been the strength of a lot of these countries which is the use of an extensive, political party as a way of keeping control over the masses.

Now, the BSPP was never really that strong—it really *was* the military that was strongest. So when they moved away from many of these practices in 1988 under the SLORC (State Law and Order Restoration Council), abandoning all of the BSPP and the ideology that came with it and becoming much more of an obvious military junta—continuing to control industries but now no longer in the name of any kind of ideology but simply as a means of financing the military—the situation became much more blatant.

But compare this to a country like Vietnam. Why has the military been so strong there? Well, in Vietnam the "revolution" was really a civil war, and the communist party got built up at the same time that military forces were trying to gain control of the country.

So you can't separate very well the military and communist party in Vietnam—therefore, the military remained strong, but always with the communist party being very strong as well; and that remains to this day.

Once you get to places like Indonesia or Thailand, the history of the armed forces and their role in politics is similar in that they had a role in the initial state creation.

The Thai military is probably the earliest modern military in Southeast Asia, having overthrown the monarchy—first in 1932 before reinstating it—but they became intrinsically linked to the evolution of businesses and economic growth in the country.

The same can be said for Indonesia. Indonesia's military was the instrument of what they called their own revolution, which basically was an anti-colonial struggle against the Dutch—but once victorious, it was recognized that they played a strong role in maintaining Indonesia's integrity and nobody really questioned that they could play some role in politics and some role in the economy.

Actually, up until today, it was even a common practice that they would have their own businesses in order to fund themselves as a supplement to state funding.

So, yes, in some ways you can say that the two places are similar in the sense that they both have very strong militaries, but these militaries exist against the backdrop of a role that they've played in society, how they've been tied to certain economic ways of organizing society, that are very different.

Questions for Discussion:

1. *In what ways can the tradition of strong militaries in Southeast Asia be regarded as a product of colonialism?*

2. *To what extent is "the rule of law" an objectively assessable concept?*

IV. The Need For Caution

Political understanding vs. a normative agenda

HB: Once again you're highlighting the important role that diversity plays in this region, how very different historical and cultural backgrounds interact with various economic, political and military factors to produce many unique trajectories.

In some ways this makes me think that this results in a wonderful laboratory to be examining various ideas and concepts. If political science is to be a science—which is a separate question to tackle, of course, that I welcome your response to—then one should be able to form theses and hypotheses, one should be able to test them, saying things like, "*Well, if this is a statement that has a certain amount of validity, statistically speaking, we should be able to check it and find evidence for it here and here.*"

And my sense is that you do this sort of thing throughout your book and I thought that it was worth pointing them out and getting your view on things.

For example, in the beginning you say something like, "*There's this understanding in modern political theory that as the middle class grows and becomes more and more prosperous this has a positive effect on stimulating increasing levels of democracy,*" so you decide to take a careful look at all these different regions to see if this was actually happening.

And my sense was, essentially, that you found out that it actually *wasn't* happening, referencing examples like Singapore and Malaysia. I mean, where are the places with the strongest middle-class?

So is there anything that we can conclude, more generally, from that? Are you at the stage where, as a political scientist, you can say something like, "*This statement which seems to be, if not a golden rule, something that at least is near-universally accepted amongst my colleagues, might actually not be that way at all"*?

Would you be willing to say something like that? I'm going to push you a little bit here in the effort to do my bit to try to actually move "political science" to becoming a real science.

JB: Well, you're asking the wrong person though to make a strong statement that political science is a really rigorous science. I believe in the endeavour of political science as a comparative endeavour and to think about factors of explanation like: *When you develop a strong middle-class, does it lead to more democracy?*

I believe that we can understand change through understanding certain factors and compare why in certain circumstances they seem to operate in the same way and then why they differ. This is a constant focus of my work: when looking at village politics in Indonesia, I compared villages; if I worked on regions, I compared regions.

So, why is it that the middle-class thesis in political science that you mentioned doesn't do very well in the study of Southeast Asia?

Well, I have two answers to this. The first is the "political science answer", which is to say that we need to add more factors of analysis that can allow us to understand the context under which the middle class will actually produce an increase in democracy.

HB: In other words, your thesis was right by definition, you just have to find a way to jig it.

JB: Well, we didn't look at enough factors that were interacting with a strong middle-class.

HB: Well, it's impossible to be falsified in other words. The argument seems to be something like, *There's no way our thesis can possibly be wrong and we just have to keep working until we find the right factors somewhere that demonstrate that it's correct.*

JB: Well, that's where political science becomes a probabilistic science. Yes, we're not going to have a theoretical proposition that holds under all circumstances—at some level the social world just doesn't work like that.

So, one way to understand the social world is to try to understand through these factors of explanation, and another is to develop a deeper understanding of the history in question to better appreciate how these factors work in a specific case, how they interact with particular cultures or political circumstances in the region or country that you're looking at.

To return to this issue of the middle class and democracy—since you explicitly raised this issue—as I said, the standard revisionist, political science view would be something like, "*We didn't actually think about many instances in which, for instance the working class has been much stronger or it's been the business elite that has been important.*"

In this view, we can see the experiences in Southeast Asia allowing us to think more carefully about what we mean, exactly, by "middle class", together with trying to get a better sense of the mechanism at play that we're concerned about here. So is it simply a case of middle-income tier professionals, students and so forth demonstrating in favour of democracy, or does it also include a segment of the business elite?

Now the business elite—and I make this point in the book—oftentimes has very different kinds of interests.

You see a business elite in Thailand becoming very favourable to democracy because a lot of the conglomerates and large corporations that were doing really well under authoritarian rule were based in Bangkok and large cities. And as you had business interests rising in rural areas and forming their different centers of interest, they were interested in opening up the spectrum and becoming, in effect, a force in favour of democracy.

But some other countries tend to be more conservative, and if the economy is favouring their interest, they tend to strongly support the government that is serving their interests.

So when you have a country such as Singapore or Malaysia, where much of the business interests are tied to the stability and continuity of the regime, they're certainly not going to be pushing in favour of change.

So that's the "business class side" of the equation, if you will. But another question that should be asked is, *How does the middle class* **on its own** *express change?*

It expresses it through political pressure of different kinds: getting involved in political parties, generally being critical, demonstrations and so forth. Which may mean that there are times when arguments of the middle classes don't get "captured politically": with more and more people active in an increasingly diverse society, they have many interests yet no political voice, no vehicle to express their voice.

In some ways, when you look at a place like Indonesia, the middle class develops like this. Why? Because you had 33 years of economic growth under the New Order regime of President Suharto but the political channels remain pretty much limited and the same.

If you joined the main government party, Golkar, and rose through its ranks, you could have a voice, but it was a very stifling environment where bringing in new ideas or trying to adapt to new situations was usually quite difficult.

That being said, the major, reformist movement that led to democratization in Indonesia actually *did* follow that trajectory, but it took 15–20 years of reformists starting to think critically from inside the regime to push and change the regime at the end.

So, a regime like Suharto's Indonesia was one that, 30 years later, was still, for instance, accusing people of communist sympathies if they opposed the government in any significant way through demonstrations in the streets, at a time when the idea that there was a "communist threat" in Indonesia was simply ludicrous.

And for the increasingly educated middle class, the rhetoric and actions of the government simply became more and more constraining, even though some of them obviously profited from the status quo from being employees of the government or involved with corporations that were associated with the regime.

If we think about Singapore and Malaysia, what distinguishes them in some ways is that so much of the middle class is tied to the regime, so when trying to understand this, we need to understand some of the unique history—in Malaysia, for instance, a history of ethnic division.

So, I'm constantly going from more unique factors to more general factors.

HB: So I very much appreciate and respect that. Moreover, I'm also deliberately trying to be a bit provocative, as I'm sure you appreciate. But I'm still bothered by aspects of this—not so much what you are saying, which all, frankly, sounds quite reasonable and well-informed to me—but by this invocation of a general thesis.

Let me try to explain my discomfort a bit more clearly. And let me begin by what I'm *not* uncomfortable with.

When you are looking carefully at individual places and examine their development as best you can in light of your knowledge of their unique history, cultural and economic factors, surrounding influences and so on, that seems completely reasonable and appropriate to me. It seems to me that you are trying to develop a framework of interpretation, a deeper understanding, of not only *how* they became what they are but what that actually means—*what*, if you like they actually *are* today and how that compares to neighbouring countries, regions, what have you.

So that's all fine. But my problem starts with those who say things like, "*A rising middle class will inevitably result in more democracy, and if we don't actually see that happening then we're not looking at the right factors for what we mean by 'rising middle class.'*"

And I have two problems with this approach. The first, as I've already said, is that it posits a deliberately non-falsifiable statement and places you in a situation where your thesis can never be rejected: you just have to sufficiently tweak your definitions and factors and so forth in order to ensure that it is true. That's more of, shall we say, a "theoretical point" about political science not being a science and all of that. But I've already hammered away at that long enough, which is probably silly for me to have been doing in the first place because, as you pointed out, *you're* not the person I should be directing that argument against anyway.

But my second point is a bit of a different one: it seems to me that hidden in this thesis there seems to be a sort of subtle condescending judgement: *"We all know what democracy is—**we** have it and many of these other places don't—and once they get their act together and start appropriately empowering the middle classes they will place themselves on a trajectory where, eventually, they will see the light and become just like us."*

And aside from my knee-jerk disdain for any such smug, triumphalist sentiments, my sense is that this represents a structural lost opportunity to look objectively at other places and see how that experience might positively affect *us*.

I mean, what's interesting to me is that in many ways these societies are *not* like ours, so rather than looking at them as "proto-European" or "proto-American", maybe there's something that we can actually *learn* from them, rather than trying to view them in that filter. Does that make any sense?

JB: Yes, it makes sense but I'd like to look at it from two, different angles.

The first angle is that, when we're trying to study political phenomena and political change, we have to have a vocabulary, we have to have something that we can compare. Although I'm sympathetic to history and sympathetic to cultural differences, what I resist is the idea that we're simply telling a *story*, because that's what happens in the end if you emphasize too much diversity.

Say you're looking at the question, *Why is it that Cambodia is in the situation that it is in now?* or, *Why is it that Burma had a military in charge and now, perhaps, it's moving towards democratic politics?*

One route to go is simply to study the intricacies of Burma itself, try to understand every particular pattern historically and, from there, to understand current circumstances. The limitation of that approach is that there's nothing really telling you how to choose what's important: why would you emphasize the military or the middle class or economic growth rates or other factors?

That's why the endeavour of political science, despite its limitations, allows us to look probabilistically at why some factors appear to work to understand certain processes.

So we think about democracy, we think about economic growth, we think about the role of elites in particular ways, we think about certain factors such as mass mobilization—mass mobilization tends to produce democratic outcomes—and understanding these processes in a comparative manner allows us to, at least, have analytical tools from which we can then see why it works and doesn't work.

That all being said, you're right that we have to be careful not to impose a normative perspective that sometimes comes with such an analysis, a perspective where we believe there's a certain trajectory that societies should take to become, for instance, democratic, in a particular way that we think is the right way.

Political science was accused thirty or forty years ago of having exactly that kind of agenda, and it comes back regularly: that a lot of scholars study democracies because they'd like to see democracy across the world.

There was a frequent debate a few years back about "the end of ideology", that all countries were inevitably going to become democratic in a, sort of, American or liberal-democratic form.

I agree that there's a danger in this kind of analysis, to think that the scholarly work has this kind of agenda behind it, but at the same time, I think one can do so with a little bit of an analytical distance.

At some level—and I tell my students this—when I'm talking about democracy, even in this book, it's within certain parameters. We don't talk about democracy in analytical terms with a whole package that comes with how we understand a particular society like Canada or the United States. There are certain parameters, certain freedoms to participate—elections that are free and fair—and rights that go with that: if you can't create freedom of association, freedom of the media, how can you have free elections?

To say that elections, per se, are actually putting a stamp on a better or different form of government is, I believe, an exaggeration. Elections are a mechanism for choosing leaders. All authoritarian states, at some point, like to call themselves "democratic"—or to at least make the point that they are accountable to their people, because the modern state is built around accountability to one's people. So whether one is communist or authoritarian, most governments make, at least in a rhetorical way, the argument that they're accountable.

HB: Perhaps it's worth clarifying one point. I'm not at all suggesting that political scientists, or anyone else for that matter, need to be scrupulously objective and non-committal.

I have no problem with you as a political scientist wanting to shout from the rooftops that, say, *Democracy is a great thing to have and that we should all be more democratic*, or that, more generally, we should all be more like *this* or less like *that*.

I don't have any problem with that whatsoever, as long as you're conducting your research in a fair, objective, reasonable, rational, scientific way, to support your claims. I'm all for opinionated scholars—life would be vastly more boring, among other things, if nobody actually held strong views or took the trouble to air them.

But what starts to rankle me personally is this descent into cliché where one is mouthing phrases and throwing words around when it's far from clear what we're talking about. So, let me try to be more specific and give you a sense of what I mean by this.

It also bears emphasizing that *you* are hardly the subject of my irritation. Indeed, while I don't claim to know you at all, from the little experience I have had of you and your ideas—via this conversation and your book on political change in Southeast Asia—you strike me as a strikingly non-dogmatic and sensitive person. So it's worth bearing in mind that my concerns are not directed at you, but rather aspects that I've detected—rightly or wrongly—from some members of your profession; and since you're the political scientist in the room I thought it appropriate to address them to you.

So what am I talking about here when I'm going on about clichés and throwing words around? Well, let's return to this notion of "democracy".

Somewhere in your book you talk about a possible sign of—I can't remember the expression exactly: "semi-democratic" or "soft-democratic" or "not fully democratic"—being the concept of gerrymandering: deliberately rejigging the electoral boundaries of a region or constituency in order to perpetuate the power of those presently in office.

And I think to myself, *Gee, that sounds just like the US Congress—they do that sort of thing all the time.*

So this makes me think, *Well, then, is the United States* **semi-democratic?** And what about the electoral college? What can you say about the democratic values of a place where the head of state can be anointed while clearly attaining *less* votes than his opponent? Or what about places like the United Kingdom or Canada when the Prime Minister can find himself at the head of a majority government—with no real checks or balances on his power whatsoever—with only, say, 40% of the popular vote? So if the United States and United Kingdom and Canada and Australia and so forth are only "semi-democratic", where exactly are the "democratic" countries?

Understand that I'm not saying that everywhere is equivalent and you might as well be in North Korea as North Carolina. That's *not* what I'm saying. But what I'm trying to point out is that it seems to me that many of these classifications that are posing as rigorous and objective actually aren't.

JB: Yes, I think it becomes problematic when we think of democracy and authoritarianism as two opposite categories. I prefer to think of it as a spectrum, with a lot in the middle, a lot of grey areas.

So, to me, if we were to ask, *"Were the Burmese people happy under the military regime?* I would have no qualms with saying, *"Of course not."*

Now, if you asked Singaporeans who lived under Lee Kuan Yew, *"Was that a regime that they could live under and find that there were advantages?"* you would find some people who would be supportive of that statement, people who would buy in to what Lee Kuan Yew in Singapore used to strongly make as his argument: that here was a tiny little island that was impoverished and, through his management, for better or worse, the society became wealthy—and, many Singaporeans who became wealthy during those years bought in to the idea that there was a trade-off.

Was it *necessary* for Singapore to have those kinds of restricted laws and tight control from the state? When I talk about gerrymandering in the book, the places with which I have the biggest problems are places like Singapore. It's one thing to gerrymander in Canada or the United States where at least you still have different parties who can win the elections, but it's another thing when you're gerrymandering to basically avoid having five or six seats go to the opposition.

HB: But you understand my point right?

JB: Yes, of course.

HB: It's a matter of degree, clearly, but I'm not sure that it's a matter of kind; and that's really my point: that we have to always be intellectually honest with ourselves not only about how we are acting, but to what extent the words we are using to describe our own actions are actually true and meaningful.

JB: We do have to be careful, yes. That's why I usually come back to the need to carefully classify as part of our analysis. We need to understand that there *are* differences between a regime in which everything is tightly controlled under military rule and a regime in which you have the freedom to say what you want, organize environmental movements, organize a free press, run for office and so forth.

When we look at Indonesia today, which is the best example of democratic politics in the region, I think many Southeast Asians would look at Indonesia and find that it's a place that they would like to live rather than, say, in the closed, impoverished, military-dominated society that Burma was for several decades.

So, those are the ends of the spectrum. It's really hard to make sense of things in the middle—of course there are trade-offs at some level, which is why, from an analytical perspective, we try to define and decide what are some of the minimal parameters that we think are important in order to understand what makes one regime democratic and one authoritarian.

And that usually revolves around free and fair elections and the rights that come along with them, in order to avoid placing what would be a template in what would be an ideal regime that we would want to see there—which was what political science was accused of in many ways of hoping for, a little too strongly perhaps, 40 years ago.

Questions for Discussion:

*1. Do you agree that the word "democracy" is not as well-defined as most people assume that it is? (Readers interested in this issue are referred to the Ideas Roadshow conversation **Democracy: Clarifying the Muddle** with University of Cambridge political theorist John Dunn.)*

2. In what ways is Jacques' previous mention of the disproportional interest in Vietnam in American political science departments as a result of the Vietnam War an indication of Howard's concerns?

*3. To what extent can political science be considered "a science"? Readers interested in this issue are referred to Chapters 2–4 of **How Social Science Creates the World** with political theorist Mark Bevir and Chapter X of **Pants on Fire: On Lying in Politics** with intellectual historian Martin Jay.*

V. Breaking Away

Dealing with secessionist movements

HB: In my mind there's a related example that struck me when I was reading your book. You talk about how, after the Suharto regime, his vice-president who replaced him, Habibie, did not win the 1999 election both because there was a banking scandal but also because he was in favour of granting independence to East Timor and allowed them to have a referendum on independence.

And the results of this referendum were strongly in favour of independence, which played a not insignificant role in him not winning the 1999 election.

So, to me that's interesting because I look at that and I compare it to what I said before about democracy. Let's forget about the banking scandal for a moment—let's assume that the election was lost solely, or at least primarily, due to this business about East Timor.

I can imagine a possible world where some reasonably progressive fellow stands up and says, *"You know what, we're going to let these guys in East Timor have their independence because they are completely different, they have a different history, religion, orientation and so forth. We invaded them, which was a mistake, and now we have to let them go since that's what they want,"* and he loses the election because of that. So I think to myself that this too represents a real problem for the concept of democracy.

JB: It does; but what's particularly interesting in that story of Habibie and why he let go of East Timor is that he would actually make that offer in the first place.

I mean, most states—and here we can talk about democracy at large—are reluctant to let go of any region. Allowing a referendum on independence and having a clear sense of what would happen—although technically the referendum was on whether or not they were going to vote for a wide range in autonomy within Indonesia, the implication was clearly that rejection was going to lead to independence—is something that has been not been easy to accept even in Canada, in Europe, in most places that we consider to be advanced democracies.

So, in fact, the phenomenon of how states deal with their ethno-nationalist or secessionalist regions in Southeast Asia, has been not completely different from most states in that they tend to want to keep those regions.

Now, what's interesting is that Indonesia has had a wide range of different responses when it comes to how it's treated its regions that are asking for more autonomy or secession. So, president Habibie let go of East Timor under pressure from the international community, which had been asking for several years that the question of East Timor be settled.

And that kind of international pressure could not be applied in any of the other secessionist conflicts that are occurring in Southeast Asia—whether it is Papua in Indonesia, Aceh also in Indonesia, the south of Thailand or the south of the Philippines—because all of these other areas are actually internationally recognized as being part of those states.

Habibie was in a difficult situation with international donors at the time, and because there had been the Asian financial crisis of 1997 he had to, in some ways, continue to have good relations as he was trying to re-stabilize the country, and international donors wanted a solution to East Timor to happen. It took all those combined forces, all that pressure, for a president in Indonesia to decide to allow a referendum on independence.

If you poll people in the Philippines, in Thailand, in Indonesia, they would all be strongly opposed to letting go of any of the secessionist regions. I think the problem is less than of secession than what kinds of compromises they're willing to give to people locally.

That's the more surprising part, and one that I think is a problem from a democratic perspective.

If you think of the regions of Papua or Aceh, for instance, for years Indonesia was built on the idea that institutions had to be homogeneous across the whole archipelago and that it was basically one state and one political system: that was the view that was officially promulgated.

But if you look at the history, Indonesia declared independence from the Dutch in 1945 and when the Dutch finally left in 1950, they still retained Papua. A little more than a decade later, the Dutch formally ceded the territory, and then there was a supposed Act of Free Choice that the United Nations ratified; and, as a result of that and because of the process in which this was done, the Papuans were integrated into Indonesia through a selection of about a hundred delegates and they felt that they had not been consulted. It was a small group that objected to this integration but they have been claiming ever since that they should have a revision internationally of this process by which they were integrated.

And today, the vast majority in Papua reject the Indonesian state. If there was a free and fair referendum, you could be sure that more than 90% of Papuans—not migrants that came from the rest of Indonesia but actual Papuans themselves—would vote in favour of independence.

They have a certain measure of autonomy, but it's an autonomy that came from an act of parliament that wasn't negotiated with representatives from Papua. They have a law "on special autonomy" that gives them a fair amount of powers and fiscal resources, but the elements of this were never really negotiated: it was a sort of "bottom-up" process that got hijacked by the parliament, and many people including the governor of the region were objecting to many aspects of it.

HB: Is that what rankles with them? Is it the process or is it actually the fact that they want more rights and more autonomy and more stuff? Or is it both?

JB: Well, they get a lot of fiscal resources, but they disappear because there's no legitimacy to this act in some way, so it hasn't been the right framework for them to reconstitute political institutions that would reflect their needs. So it's subject to a lot more corruption and inefficiencies; effectively there's a lack of implementation because there's no buy-in from the Papuans and the Indonesian state is not committed to making it work very well.

Now contrast that with Aceh, which obtained a very extensive autonomy law that was negotiated with the "Free Aceh Movement" after it was in a war with the Indonesian state. And after the ceasefire, they ended up having a very elaborate law after having sat down and negotiated a lot of the terms.

So of those groups that have been mobilizing for more autonomy or secession, the Acehnese have actually obtained the most in terms of institutions, fiscal resources and any recognition of their differences within Indonesia. Even though Indonesia is a very different place, they obtained some sort of special status that has allowed them to basically feel that they can be part of Indonesia on the terms that they wanted to be part of Indonesia.

HB: And, is there an understanding of that within the Indonesian government right now? If you were having a conversation with the current president of Indonesia and asked him, "*Would you recognize that there were places that you treated some secessionist movements better and others worse,*" would he reply to you, "*Yes, you're right; we should do a better job with that and I'm working on that,*" or would there be a denial?

JB: I think they would agree with that, yes. Both Joko Widodo, the new president, and SBY, the outgoing president, have agreed that there needed to be some improvements in Papua and there needed to be some reworking of the law; but I think that there's a worry in their mind that if you give too much, especially in Papua, they will ask for independence.

So, there really is that concern about giving a platform to secessionists, whereas they didn't have that fear as much with Aceh. And probably because the history of injustice in Papua—or at least perceived injustice in terms of integration—is something they'll have trouble getting over because the secessionists want the international community to reopen that question; and I think ultimately there's a concern that increased local power would be used as a platform to revisit the process of integration.

That all being said, it's a trend in the region that the central government will say that they understand the concerns but then there's not a whole lot that gets done.

For instance, in the Philippines there has been a conflict with the Muslims in the south of the Philippines that goes back several decades; and under democratic government there was a first cease-fire agreement in 1996, which led to one of the organizations fighting against the state agreeing to sign a peace agreement with the state, but that got poorly implemented as well.

After that, another organization rose and took its place; and it's only very recently that the government now has signed an agreement to try to form a new autonomous region with new powers.

What do you do when you're in the state of the Philippines in which implementing laws is oftentimes, difficult? They've passed a lot of laws but the laws don't get implemented very well.

The Philippines is a democracy but a democracy that is not functioning very well and that's clearly visible when the laws are poorly implemented. But when you're trying to develop a framework to accommodate demands from a group like the Moros and a consequent recognition of an autonomous region, it's important that these laws get implemented properly and that the promises made by both sides are actually implemented.

HB: Do you think that secessionist movements in this region will get stronger, on the whole? Are you prepared to make any generalizations at all?

JB: I don't think one can make generalizations because there's a whole spectrum of circumstances.

I can say that I don't think there are going to be more secessionist movements than the ones that are already there. Each one of them has a fairly long history of why they became secessionist. I've already mentioned Papua's history of integration. Aceh, as I said, had other specificities. In the south of Thailand it's really a cultural, religious difference: they're Malay, they're Muslim, and their rights as both Malays and Muslims have really been curtailed. In the Philippines, there was a sense of marginalization and displacement of Muslims, such as the Moro Muslims in the south that I've just spoken about, where claims to both land and to recognition of Muslim institutions is important.

These are fairly long histories of regionally-based groups that had a history of grievances. When you think of other regions, for the most part, they've been well-integrated in the states in which they belong. Indonesia tends to be an example of a country that, successfully, was able to recognize difference while creating some sense of unity. That got abused under authoritarian rule but really the basis of the Indonesian state—recognizing different languages, recognizing different cultural groups, but then creating a core around the Indonesian language and the common history—has been fine for most groups in Indonesia.

So there really are no additional pressures for secession.

The only other country that still has a very deep set of issues is Burma. But Burma doesn't have a clear coincidence between territorial concentration and its ethnic groups, so it becomes very complex when thinking about whether these groups would demand secession or not.

Many of them are scattered in different areas through a combination of their individual histories and settlement processes, the impact of colonialism, displacement through war and so on.

There are some states that are recognized for certain ethnic groups—like the Shan State—but on the whole it's still quite mixed. For some groups, like the Karen—it would be very difficult to identify a clear, Karen geographic area whereas it would be easier for other groups.

So, the Burmese are having enormous difficulty thinking through, in this emerging democracy, how they will be able to accommodate their ethnic diversity. Will it be through recognizing certain provinces? Having a federal system? Will there be political parties? It's a bit of an unknown.

HB: Is it actually, in your view, an emerging democracy? Is there genuine will towards becoming, eventually, a normal, standard democracy at the end of the day, or is this just window-dressing to be able to allow the junta more time to cling to power?

JB: Nobody can really read very well the military in Burma. So, anything is speculative as to what kind of debates are occurring within the junta. Clearly, it came as a surprise when the junta suddenly decided it had to take a democratic route.

There are two ways of seeing this.

One could see it as being a very carefully planned process that started early in the 2000s where they actually did announce that they were going to have a reform process, and for years, they were discussing, even with the opposition, Aung San Suu Kyi and her party, a new constitution. Now, the NLD and Aung San Suu Kyi withdrew from those discussions early on, but that process continued and that's where we are now: the constitution has been put into place and then they opened up.

On the other hand, the other way to see it is that, irrespective of that process, it still came as a surprise that they're opening up as much as they are, that this arose from an internal erosion—economically and institutionally—resulting from a great deal of external pressure—sanctions and so forth—that made it very difficult for the Burmese military to continue to manage the emerging protests that were occurring in Burma.

The "Saffron Revolution" got them very nervous: if Buddhist monks were now demonstrating in the streets, it meant that they were facing more and more people who would be ready to demonstrate because of poor economic conditions; and the sanctions that the West imposed were starting to hurt more and more.

So there are some views that it was the result of these kinds of sanctions, internal erosion, and demonstrations that triggered this desire to open up.

Now, that being said, Thein Sein is seen as a reformer, but without doubt there are many more who wish that the process doesn't continue advancing as quickly as it has been going.

HB: So, what do *you* think the motivations were for what has happened? You've very skillfully set up the differing views, but let me ask you to speculate a bit. What are your gut feelings?

JB: Well, my gut feeling is that the military regime felt that it would just be facing more and more demonstrations. Increasing numbers of Burmese were demonstrating on a regular basis since 1988 and the military junta lost the ideological reasons why it was in power: it was basically serving the interests of the military.

It created a capital city that was simply serving the armed forces, and there wasn't much of a future possibility for anyone other than simply joining the armed forces.

And at some point, they couldn't continue absorbing more people into the armed forces as a future growth policy: they had to be able to economically allow the country to advance.

HB: Wasn't this capital city just created in the middle of nowhere because some army guy's astrologer told him that's where they should put it?

JB: That's right, yes. So I think that the armed forces probably just came to the end of their rope: they couldn't continue having the kind of closed society and control over the economy and polity without giving a chance for others to take part in some sort of political change or economic change.

Now, that being said, the constitution very much maintains the role of the military. The constitution that was put into place was inspired by the model that the military used in Indonesia as its way of ruling. In other words, I think they want a controlled level of change:

they want to be able to absorb the opposition in some ways but they don't want to relinquish control.

Questions for Discussion:

1. Why do you think the international political pressure on Indonesia to grant independence to East Timor was so strong? What were the factors that led to this pressure?

2. To what extent has the geographical dispersion of the Karen people that Jacques highlights resulted in a greater threat to their survival than other ethnic groups?

VI. Asian Values

Rhetorical trope or meaningful distinction?

HB: I'd like to talk for a moment about the notion of "Asian values". This was something that was all the vogue about twenty years ago or so, I think—promulgated, at least in my recollection, most loudly by people like Lee Kuan Yew who effectively announced that all of these things that the West maintains are absolutely necessary for the development of a modern state is just one way of doing things and that Asians do things in a different way as they are different people and have different cultural values and so forth.

These sorts of statements were assailed by a wide variety of people who said that they were just a front for being able to transgress universal human rights while clinging on to power by appealing to a base sort of "ethnic populism".

Personally, I'm quite willing to believe aspects of this, but I'm not sure it makes sense to disregard the whole argument holus-bolus. But what do you think? As somebody who has studied Southeast Asia in great detail and throughout a wide variety of different countries and different cultural groups, can you say that there are some commonalities, there is some uniqueness to what it means to be, at least, Southeast Asian, if not Asian in general?

JB: I think the argument that cultural difference needs to be taken seriously when creating a democratic society is important and that can justify a lot of differences. I think one of the reasons why "the Asian values" debate disappeared is that it was primarily regarded as a rhetorical device more than anything else, but I wouldn't go as far as to say that there's nothing to it.

If anything, in my view, there are many Asian values—they tend to vary from country to country and they're certainly different from what you see in Europe or North America, but they express themselves very differently.

Why it didn't work to be able to position "Asian values" as one model that would be different from the West is that there was no consistent set of either prescriptions or values that one can look at.

So, for Lee Kuan Yew, it came down to a justification as to why it would be important to have a society that's led through choosing economic growth over political freedom; and if he teased out his thoughts, a lot of what you would find is him delving into certain values that might resonate in a Confucian-inspired society.

Again, that became very controversial: Does a patrimonial society *really* reflect Confucian values? Does authority or order over freedom *really* reflect the Confucian ethic? Those who are studying Confucianism would say that you can choose a number of different values in Confucianism and they won't necessarily be in the order that Lee Kuan Yew would have liked to see them. There are scholars such as Daniel Bell working on Confucianism in China, looking at the democratic roots of Confucianism and ideas of freedom.

So, my sense is that it was useful as a way to try to position societies such as Singapore and other places—Matahir Mohamad in Malaysia was quite in agreement with this sort of rhetorical device as well—to reject the kind of homogeneous view of democratic politics with freedom of political participation as the ultimate value over and above economic growth and economic development.

From their perspective, the thinking was, *If you have to make that choice*—and the question is: ***do you?*** Perhaps not—*maybe people will choose to develop and have economic growth, even if it means that they don't have political participation and political freedom.*

Now, he didn't poll Singaporeans to ask them, nor did Matahir in Malaysia—and it's only post hoc that you can say that there was both a lot of criticism and a lot of support for both leaders.

But perhaps certain aspects of this might be relevant today. If you look at an emerging democracy such as Indonesia, Islam plays a naturally important role, but that was also part of the rhetoric of "Asian values"—it wasn't just Confucian-based societies, there is this whole part of Southeast Asia which is basically Muslim and has nothing to do with Confucianism.

The largest Muslim country in the world is Indonesia; and the good news about Indonesia is that there seems to be an ability to have elections, to have freedom of press, freedom of association and many others while having a debate internally about what it means to be an Islamic society or what it means to be a Muslim-majority society. People were able to publicly consider questions such as, *How can we integrate Muslim values while respecting the values of non-Muslims, while respecting certain kinds of democratic practices?*

This means that in some of the legislation that will come out, they might seem more restrictive than here—for example, their pornography laws are going to be a lot more restrictive than those here. But the point is that this creates a debate of many issues, and they're capable of having such a debate within a democratic framework, and then they come out with laws that some people may not be happy about, but at least they've been debated to some extent.

HB: It seems to me that, even though most people are no longer using the words "Asian Values," the argument about choosing or prioritizing between economic growth and political freedom is very much an active one these days, particularly when it comes to China.

When they're looking at China they're effectively saying, "Here is this enormously powerful and huge state that is undergoing this remarkably rapid societal-wide transformation, and they are doing it in a way which certainly does not mesh with all of the fundamental principles that we promulgate here in the West."

So the question is, *Are they making some huge mistake? Should they be doing things differently, somehow? Is it somehow necessary to do it this way given their particular circumstances?* And then, perhaps, *What, if anything, do their experiences imply about the way we should be doing things?*

JB: Well, here's the dilemma when you don't have a democracy. If you don't have a debate, how do you know that you're on the right kind of path—or, at least, the path that reflects your society and the choices that you have to make?

There are many arguments that one can make regarding China. China has a long history of states that collapsed: it's a place that's historically been very, very difficult to manage. So one can, in all humility, say that just keeping China together is a feat because there are so many people and it's such a large place; and that could be one argument that one might theoretically use to say something like, *If you opened up the kettle and had democratic politics, you might not be able to continue to have the kind of prosperity that's happening in China.*

But that prosperity is coming at a considerable cost: there are many human rights abuses, and now we're seeing creeping debate in China over environmental issues because pollution levels have become so high that they're getting a lot of demonstrations and riots.

So the question is: *What are the mechanisms that allow people to have a debate with their government?* And if you're too restricted, you can't make a choice.

Coming back to Lee Kuan Yew—it's easy for leaders *after* the fact, when they're showing their accomplishments of high levels of economic growth, to make the claim that, "*It could not have been otherwise.*"

And maybe, in fact, they're right. But we don't know; and there hasn't been the chance for society to debate it.

HB: There's also, I think, this notion of "the human condition", which isn't simply a nice phrase trotted out by historians or anthropologists or whatever, it is also instantiated in things like the Universal Declaration of Human Rights. And this idea of the commonality of the human experience—a fundamental sense of egalitarianism which can be expressed at its base level by notions such as: all human lives are equally valuable and meaningful—is always to some extent in opposition to this notion of cultural distinctiveness and diversity.

Let me try, then, to be a bit more concrete: when I look at South-east Asia, for example, I'm struck by the fact that there seems to be, as you said earlier, a tremendous amount of diversity—culturally, historically, politically and so forth—and yet, at the same time, I'm wondering if there might be some aspects of commonality that exist between various different countries in the region compared to places in North America or Europe, say.

What do you think? Does it even make sense to talk about cultural values within Southeast Asia? Is that even an intellectually coherent idea?

JB: I don't think that we can talk about cultural values on a Southeast Asian-wide level because there are too many differences in Southeast Asia. The cultural differences will be just as great between countries in Southeast Asia as they might be between some countries in South-east Asia and Canada, say—with one exception perhaps. They're all more religious-oriented societies than you would find here.

Religion is taken seriously in all of these societies, but there are different religions. So, yes—to the extent that you can find common values that come out of a highly devout Catholic society in the Philip-pines and a highly devout Muslim society in Indonesia and Malaysia—perhaps you'll find some common, human values that are expressed in religious form, and that at some level imbue some of the politics of the region.

It is important to many of the countries in the region that religion be sponsored and supported by the state, whereas we're not favour-able to that kind of view in the West at all: we believe very strongly in the separation between church and state. That's one commonality in Southeast Asia where you wouldn't find many people thinking that the state has no space in religion.

HB: Well, we believe that *now*. But two-hundred or three-hundred years ago, it was quite different.

JB: Exactly.

But aside from that there aren't a whole lot of clear commonalities on a regional level. There are sub-groups. You certainly have the debate within countries such as Malaysia and Indonesia that I spoke about earlier about how far to go in recognizing Islamic values and implementing them in legislation while having democratic politics.

Indonesia shines, in the Muslim world, in its ability to have a certain level of open politics that's stable and allows for that level of societal debate.

Thailand is a unique place too. Often the issue there is less about Buddhism per se than how Buddhism is represented in the monarchy—the monarchy is the head of state, it's the symbol of the nation. And so, because there has been controversy over the political power that people around the king have had, that has led to *very serious* divisions internally, involving—among other things— attempts to bring some of the masses that were in poor and marginalized parts of Thailand into the political spectrum.

What we're seeing now in Thailand began with the election of Prime Minister Thaksin: he mobilized vast numbers of people in rural areas who had never been fully incorporated into the political process and he brought them in to support his party, challenging the power of the middle class in Bangkok and those who were around the king, thereby dividing the society very significantly.

In some ways, one can see this as a realpolitik situation: *What are you going to tap into in order to maintain power?*

But on the other hand, Thailand, as a country that came out of a long history without colonialism where the monarch *was* the important figure, continued to be in modern Thailand, and represents both religion *and* state, this challenge tends to threaten the state at different levels.

It's not just a question of politics. At that point, you're also threatening what the monarch, as the expression of Buddhist values, has on all of Thai society.

The deep crisis is both about a realpolitik situation—who's going to win out in the end—and also a question of how much the king and Buddhism are part of the Thai nation—which also, incidentally, comes back to some of the secessionist issues we were mentioning earlier: why Thailand is the state that had the most amount of difficulty accommodating its Malay Muslim south, because the very symbols of the state come together in "king, nation and Buddhism" in a way that accommodating a Malay Muslim south contradicts what it is to be a Thai nation. Which is why, up until now, discussions of autonomy have been non-existent for the Malay.

Questions for Discussion:

1. *Do you believe the phrase "Asian values" has any real meaning? (Readers interested in this issue are referred to Chapter 4 of **Turning the Mirror: A View From the East** with author Pankaj Mishra and Chapter 10 of **Byzantium: Beyond the Cliché** with historian Maria Mavroudi.)*

2. *To what extent do you feel issues of substance are actually meaningfully debated in most Western democratic countries?*

VII. Making Progress

Knowing when to push, and when not to

HB: Given the degree of diversity, complexity and subtlety in this region, I could imagine that someone in your position would regularly be quite frustrated by the sorts of simplistic frameworks that are often imposed by those on the outside. I'm thinking particularly about the "Western media", for lack of a better term.

I'm guessing that when you read an article in the newspaper or watch something on CNN about these areas, there is frequently a sense of frustration of a lack of understanding or awareness of the complexity of the real situation on the ground? Is that, in fact, the case? Do you find that most parts of Southeast Asia are not represented faithfully, sufficiently and sensitively by the mainstream media in terms of conveying the subtleties of the issues at play, or am I off-base there?

JB: I think the biggest issue I have with media is the underreporting of Southeast Asia in comparison to other regions. Whether it's good news or bad news, you get so few stories, at least if we look at reporting in Europe or North America about Southeast Asia relative to events that are happening in many other regions in the world.

We get so much press on the Israeli-Palestinian conflict and many of the failures of the Arab Spring, which is a constant theme that we're finding in the press that continues to reinforce the view that, somehow, there's something fundamentally wrong with Muslim societies.

And then along comes a democratically, well-run election with very little violence occurring in the world's largest Muslim country and you only get one or two articles that mention it.

Now those articles are usually accurate, but the net effect of this imbalance of attention is that it skews perceptions about something as fundamental as the role of Islam in the world today.

So that is my biggest gripe with the current circumstances: really how Islam is being portrayed in the media; and it's very much defined by events in the Middle East and on where violence is most prone to be happening, where intolerance is greatest and where countries are failing—and it gives this perception that Islam is a highly intolerant, conflict-prone religion.

On the other hand, in Southeast Asia you have Indonesia and Malaysia. Malaysia's not a democratic society but it has a lot of freedoms: they are certainly not implementing Sharia law in a way that one would associate with in the Middle East or in Afghanistan or elsewhere.

These are not societies that, even in an authoritarian or semi-authoritarian setting such as Malaysia, are not exactly implementing any harsh, criminal law policies as a result of being an Islamic society or anything of this sort.

As it happens, within Malaysia, there's a lot of debate about what it means to be in a society where Islam is the religion of the state, and yet there's a free and flowing debate about the choices that people want to have in terms of restrictions or fewer restrictions or more restrictions. In fact, there are not many restrictions on living in Malaysia in relation to what one needs to wear or many of the other abuses we see in terms of women's rights or other rights in some of the news stories.

And Indonesia, of course, is a society where many of these issues get debated.

HB: So, why do you think that is? Why do you think that the media are so intent on portraying Islam in this one particular, tension-filled, sensationalist way, "Clash of Civilizations" sort of way? Is it because of historical precedent—being naturally geared to look at some parts of the world rather than others?

Is it because of a more sensationalist orientation towards focusing on conflagration as opposed to covering peaceful elections that might be happening? Is it intellectual laziness? Or is there something more sinister going on?

I mean, that strikes me as a pretty significant point you just made: here is a country of roughly two-hundred and fifty million people, the vast majority of whom are Muslim, who seem to be peaceful, democratizing, reasonably prosperous or at least moving in an increasingly prosperous way, not sabre-rattling, not threatening their neighbours, not having religious wars here, there and everywhere and yet, you would think that, in a global debate about the role of Islam in the twenty-first century, that should be front and center as an important piece of evidentiary reasoning.

However, it seems to be largely missing, so that would seem to prompt the obvious question, *"Why is that not happening?"*

JB: Well, I think that, at some level, the media *does* go where the stories are the most sensationalist. Obviously where there is deep conflict, where there is war, it will tend to gravitate toward there; and, in some ways, since the Vietnam war, there hasn't been that sort of conflict.

Of course there have been occasional, deep conflicts—obviously the Khmer Rouge in Cambodia and the period of intense killings there were also reported at the time—but by the time you get to the 1980s, aside from periodic episodes of civil war in Cambodia that were reported, many of the countries in the rest of the region didn't have the kinds of deep-seated conflicts that tend to draw the media's attention.

Part of this is just the nature of the beast: the media goes where there's a story to tell, and a good news story is rarely one that the media picks up on over war and conflict.

Secondly, I think because of the few decades where you didn't have sustained conflict in a region like Southeast Asia meant that you didn't have reporters in places that are as deeply committed to a region as, say, the Middle East where they understand the culture and so forth.

So, the result is that when you come to an issue like "the role of Islam" today, it would take an enormous amount of will to go against the "obvious stories" that are emerging and make for more sensational reading; and because of the fact that the reporters are already there on the ground, it becomes a self-perpetuating phenomenon.

HB: Right, it's a vicious circle. I have one more question. Given the considerable amount of work that you've done in diagnosing and assessing a wide variety of different places in this particular part of the world and recognizing various strengths, limitations and weaknesses, what should be done, in your view, from the Western perspective, in terms of communication, trade, diplomacy, and so forth?

If you were President Obama, say, how might you be engaging with various places in Southeast Asia differently? What sorts of things would you be doing and where? I guess what I'm really asking is: what are we not doing well, and what are we not doing well enough in terms of assisting, supporting and generally understanding Southeast Asia?

JB: Well, Southeast Asia is a difficult region to engage, both bilaterally *and* multilaterally. ASEAN is not a very cohesive or strong institution, but one of the principles that they have within ASEAN is this principle of non-interference in other people's affairs—which is an international principle in many ways—but they elevated it to another level.

HB: They made it explicit.

JB: Yes, they made it explicit, which means that they've agreed—whether it's in multilateral forms or even with relations between one another—to oppose attempts by others to put pressure on the way in which they handle their societies politically.

What that means is that, what we've seen an increased amount of in the last twenty years—pressure by countries like the United

States, Canada and others on human rights and minority rights issues tended to happen somewhat less frequently within an ASEAN context.

However, within ASEAN and even internationally, Burma was an interesting example of some change occurring in this respect. They went very carefully with Burma—there was a lot of objection internationally to bring Burma into ASEAN on the basis that Burma was a military regime that mistreated its people, Western sanctions were imposed, and there was a boycott—and it's actually through the ASEAN's softer approach of bringing Burma in that it gave an ability for the junta to actually start reintegrating into a multilateral forum, which therefore helped some of the bilateral relations.

So I think that we're seeing the kinds of changes that are happening in Burma right now mainly because there's been this kind of acceptance of evolving on the terms of the reformers combined with a slow-moving but supportive process.

And by accepting that it's not a perfect process and by engaging and supporting the changes that are being made as opposed to requesting more and pushing for more rapid change, it's actually having a positive result. I think that, politically, the example of Burma is proving that it's the best example for political reform in the region, it's really this, sort of, slow engagement.

HB: So, that's what we've done well—or, at least, what ASEAN's done well. What do we need to do better, if anything? Is there anything concrete that the West or international organizations can do better to more positively impact the region or certain specific locales within it?

JB: In terms of economic development, there's a lot of talk about the Trans-Pacific Partnership or many other kinds of forums in which there's more discussion about economic relations in the region.

In fact, the more the region is integrated in the international system and sees an interest in economic growth for their own country within this type of international context, the more likely it is to lead to positive political change.

I think we should continue to encourage Vietnam's economic reforms—Cambodia we could push a little harder—but the problem comes back to what I was saying before: you can't push very hard.

We tried to push in Cambodia and the United Nations basically failed in Cambodia: it tried to impose a UN-sponsored, democratic model after the civil war in Cambodia, which ended up failing because there was not enough of an effective institutional framework established to allow a democratic process to simply function normally.

They were still deeply divided—the Khmer Rouge were still there—it was very ambiguous as to how you could bring them in or not within the process; the opposition political parties had very little resources, very little power and they were extremely unsympathetic to cooperating with Hun Sen and the Cambodian People's Party. So, the fact then that you already had one dominant player in place could monopolize the democratic process until today.

Cambodia is always the example within ASEAN that external pressure or an attempt to oppose institutions from outside didn't work. It did in East Timor to some extent—that was a very different kind of setting—but Cambodia is usually seen as an example of the failure of UN-intervention, but the flip side is that this, sort of, gradual engagement in Burma I was just talking about, *has* been working.

I would *like* to say that if we encouraged more reform with respect to minority issues, human rights issues and the development of autonomous institutions in Papua, for example, or strongly supported the Moro Islamic Liberation Front's peace agreement with the Philippine state to work we could make a difference.

These institutions need support and the international community is aware of this, but the problem is always how much support you provide in terms of advice and resources before you get accused by the local government of "too much interference", so we're always moving somewhat gingerly.

For the most part, I'm not very critical of the policies that have been adopted towards the region.

HB: Both today and in your book, you refer regularly to Indonesia as a shining light of democracy in the region, describing how it started moving very significantly along that path "when conditions became right for democracy" as you put it.

I think the example you just gave now about the intervention in Cambodia demonstrates, as you were specifically mentioned, that the conditions were not right for democracy then, so perhaps someone who wants to attempt to exert any leverage whatsoever—it's done—has to first recognize whether or not this structural appropriateness first exists on the ground. Is that a fair statement?

JB: I think we're getting more and more examples. In fact, while Cambodia was for some time regarded as a paradigmatic case of a failure of UN-intervention, today it would be probably ranked considerably less of a failure in comparison to the likes of Iraq and Libya.

So, we end up with a host of examples that demonstrate how intervening in societies to try to build democratic institutions is very difficult to make them work. What does it mean to be right?

I make the argument in the book that we still think that a certain level of prosperity and presence of middle class is some sort of core factor that is supportive of having a democracy, but other places have been able to democratize and remain democratic despite being poor and not necessarily having a strong middle class.

You get examples like the Philippines, which has been democratic in its own way for a long time, despite being one of the least successful countries economically when compared to Indonesia and Thailand and others. It's catching up now, but for a long time it wasn't.

So, I think an important lesson learned is that a ingredient required to support democratic processes is a little bit of modesty.

East Timor certainly could have gone either way: there was no choice but to intervene there, because there was a referendum; and the problem was that the segment of the armed forces in Indonesia refused the results and they cooperated with local militias to basically destroy a good part of East Timor.

So, when left with no choice but to intervene it's a different story—in fact, there the problem was too little too late: the UN should have come much earlier and in greater force to prevent the kind of destruction that occurred in East Timor.

But once they were in place, UN forces were very helpful in creating the democratic institutions that are now in place in East Timor.

HB: Well, that's great, Jacques—thank you so much for your time and all your clear, thoughtful, measured responses. Is there anything else that you'd like to add?

JB: No, I don't think so. Thank you.

Questions for Discussion:

1. *How has this book influenced your view on "the role of Islam in the world today"? Do you agree with Jacques that the Muslim nations of Indonesia and Malaysia are largely underrepresented in this discussion?*

2. *Is it possible to counteract the media's natural orientation summarized by, "If it bleeds, it leads"?*

3. *To what extent does the international community "learn from its failures"?*

Continuing the Conversation

Readers are encouraged to read Jacques' book, *Political Change in Southeast Asia*, which goes into considerable additional detail about many of the issues discussed here.

The Power of Sympathy

Politics and Moral Sentimentalism

A conversation with Michael Frazer

Introduction

More Than Reasonable

Like most people, had you asked me to name a synonym for the Enlightenment, doubtless the first word to come to mind would have been "rationality". Of course, "the Enlightenment" means many things to many people—replacing religious superstition with scientific thinking, destroying social hierarchies, establishing comprehensive public educational efforts—but through all of its myriad incarnations, from "The Moderate Enlightenment" to "The Radical Enlightenment", from Newton's inspiring legacy to Diderot's groundbreaking encyclopedia, the one constant seems to be an overarching belief in the power of rational inquiry to enable humans to unlock their full potential.

But it turns out that that's hardly the whole story.

In his book, *The Enlightenment of Sympathy*, political philosopher Michael Frazer describes another, quite different, type of Enlightenment that is by no means uniquely guided by an emphasis on rationality, but nonetheless follows closely in the footsteps of the spirit of Immanuel Kant's influential essay, "What is Enlightenment?"

> *"Kant defines enlightenment as us overcoming our immaturity and being able to think for ourselves. Sapere aude—dare to be wise—he says. That's the motto of enlightenment: dare to think for yourself.*

> *"In the book I call that "reflective autonomy": the idea of thinking for yourself, reflecting on your own preexisting moral and political commitments and coming to evaluate them, only accepting them if they can survive that process of reflection and rejecting anything that can't.*

"But just because you're committed to reflective autonomy doesn't mean that you're committed to any one particular theory of what that reflection should involve."

Well, you might be tempted to wonder, what else can there possibly be? If I'm thinking for myself, I must be reasoning; and if I'm reasoning, I must be using my rational faculties.

But that, says Michael, makes the false equivalence between "thinking" and "reasoning", an equivalence that the likes of David Hume, Adam Smith, Johann Gottfried Herder and others of the "sentimentalist Enlightenment" tradition emphatically rejected.

"There's a kind of democratic egalitarianism of the soul in the picture of autonomous reflection that Hume and Smith and Herder and other sentimentalists put forward.

"It's still very much 'dare to be wise', sapere aude, question everything, come to your own conclusions, think for yourself. But now that "thinking" isn't something that you do with only one element of your psychology as opposed to other elements of your psychology. It's a process by which you draw on all of these various faculties.

"For them, the faculty that holds it all together, especially socially, isn't reason, it's sympathy. And sympathy itself is given different anatomies, different accounts of how it works. It usually can't be understood in terms of reason or emotion or imagination alone—imagination being another important faculty.

"I think the best account of it is the one we find in Adam Smith, where it involves a kind of imaginative projection onto someone else's situation, working out what to feel if we were them in that situation, comparing what they're actually feeling and doing to what we would feel or do, and then trying to bring those things into equilibrium with one another.

"It's the fact that we crave sympathy with one another, that there's nothing we want more than for others to sympathize with us and we want to sympathize with others: that's the glue that holds it all together, socially."

Well, it's always refreshing to learn that your preconceptions and historical understanding are decidedly more limited than they should be. So the Enlightenment wasn't just—or certainly wasn't always just—about rationality after all. It turns out that there were many thoughtful and influential people, like David Hume and Adam Smith, who interpreted things far more broadly than the standard picture leads us to believe. That's good to know.

But Michael's interest in these "sentimentalist" views is hardly limited to enriching our appreciation of history. The subtitle to, *The Enlightenment of Sympathy*, after all, is "Justice and the Moral Sentiments in the Eighteenth Century and Today". For Michael, then, there is something very important about these often-overlooked perspectives that we would do well to pay attention to in order to deepen our contemporary sociopolitical understanding.

When I suggested to him that our current age of large-scale emotional manipulation and populist demonizing might argue for a market *increase* in rational thinking at the expense of notions of "sentiment", he was quick to respond.

"The real-world upshot of this book is, 'No, that's a terrible mistake. The only way to combat emotional immaturity and selfishness is through emotional maturity, sympathy, compassion, and empathy.

"If we're to overcome those emotional tendencies that we have, especially during times of fear or uncertainty, to withdraw into our own narrow perspectives as much as possible, the only resources we have that effectively pull people back out of that aren't pure rational argument.

"They are grounded in rhetorical appeals to our power, to emotionally connect with people different from ourselves. The best political rhetoric is often very, very emotional, but it's a call to the compassionate sharing of emotion, rather than a call to narrow self-centred fear, let alone hatred. I think it's very, very important.

"Too often rhetoric gets identified with emotional manipulation, but there's a kind of emotional evocation that isn't manipulative, but

presents people with the realities of others' lived experiences and calls on people to identify with and concern themselves with those emotional experiences.

"And the highest pieces of political rhetoric are the ones that expand people's circles for the pursuit of something good, and rally them to oppose themselves to something that would narrow those circles.

"So political philosophy can get very abstract and very disconnected from political practice. But I think there are very important takeaway points for political practice from an appreciation of the sentimentalist tradition."

A very well-reasoned and sensible analysis, I must say—eminently rational, even. But not just that.

The Conversation

I. New York Origins

A very Woody Allen beginning

HB: I'd like to start off by going way back and asking you about your intellectual motivations and orientations when you were young. Were you interested in philosophical, ethical and political issues when you were a boy?

MF: I very much was—and there are a number of streams that go into that. We were speaking earlier about meritocracy, and the main thing that set me on my intellectual trajectory had to do with my schooling.

I grew up in New York and they have a system of exam-based magnet schools there. The one I'm talking about is called Hunter. The kids who grew up in Manhattan could go to the elementary school there based on an IQ test at the age of four.

And of course we envied them in the outer boroughs. I had an hour-long commute from the North Bronx, and they naturally didn't want four year olds commuting.

So the rest of us had to take a test in sixth grade at the age of 11 or so to get in. And so I started commuting into Manhattan to this school that was very intense, free, but outside of the board of education. And I've been surrounded by those same people ever since: they kept showing up. They went to college with me, and grad school with me, and they're in powerful positions in academia.

And it was a very intense, dorky place. I think probably our most famous alum who I knew was Lin-Manuel Miranda who wrote the musical *Hamilton*.

I actually wrote a play in senior year that was directed by Chris Hayes, who's now a pundit and has a show on MSNBC, and Lin was the assistant director.

HB: So do you still have contact with both of them?

MF: Well, I haven't seen much of those two in particular, generally speaking people do stay in some sort of contact throughout the rest of their lives: you're essentially admitted to the meritocracy at the age of 11, rather than at the age of 18 as happens when you get into a prestigious university, and you just sort of follow it through.

Twenty of us were undergraduates together at Yale, then three or four people were getting their PhDs—often in political theory—with me at Princeton. We actually got less money per pupil than a standard New York public high school. But the students did so much on their own. For example, we got the debate coach at a fancy private school, Collegiate, to have a joint team for Hunter and Collegiate, because Hunter couldn't pay for a debate coach.

He had a big impact on us—for a long time he worked for George Soros to promote debate in the former Soviet block. The idea was that if you have high school kids debating competitively, that's a way to promote open discourse.

HB: For an "open society".

MF: Exactly—well, you know Soros loves his open society. But that really was the effect it had on us. And he took us down for three weeks of training one summer to American University in Washington, staying in the dorms there and hanging out in DC. And he took us through the canon of political philosophy, from Plato to Rawls, in three weeks at a high-school level.

And we would spend mornings going through the texts, and afternoons having debates based upon them. It's amazing how many people I went through that experience with who are now professional philosophers or political theorists.

So this debate coach had a lot of influence, and then I had a fantastic teacher in European history who had us all roll up our trousers and pretend to be Enlightenment philosophers for a mock salon. And I dressed up as Hume at the time.

HB: Even then?

MF: Even then. And the reason I chose Hume for that exercise in European history class, was because the debate coach had us first reading Hume, because there was a standard mode of argumentation that you heard a lot in high-school debate, a kind of literalist version of the social contract.

So you'd be debating something like whether or not protection from bigotry outweighs the value of freedom of speech. And they would say things like, "*We all signed a social contract where we agreed to give up certain rights in exchange for certain protections. Therefore, we give up some of our right to freedom of speech*"—these kinds of very flat-footed social contract arguments.

And our coach basically gave us Hume's essay on refuting the idea of a social contract. In that essay, he describes how we're born into society and there's nowhere else to go—it's not like there's a state of nature, somewhere else that we can just rejoin anytime you become dissatisfied.

So the governing metaphor of that essay Hume uses is that that's like saying, if you're asleep and then captured and put on a ship and then told by the captain when you awake, "*OK, you've now tacitly agreed to be a member of my crew. You can always leave if you want to, but the only place to go is to jump into the sea.*"

Of course, later in the history of political philosophy, there are various ways to use the social contract idea that don't depend on a literalist understanding of agreement that *we actually have factually agreed to the obligations we incur as members of society.*

Rawls uses a social contract as a hypothetical, as a thought experiment, to think what we would agree to. It's not as if the idea of a social contract ceases to be useful, but this kind of flat-footed literal social contract idea is just completely devastated by the arguments that Hume makes in his essay on the topic.

HB: And you were exposed to this at quite a young age.

MF: Yes, a very young age.

HB: So presumably this helped you to develop strong critical thinking skills: you were presented with clear examples of how, just because some famous guy says X, there are ways of penetratingly critiquing that position.

MF: Reasons for saying not X. Exactly.

HB: Exactly. So I understand via a really good teacher in European history, via a very intellectually dynamic academic environment and middle school, perhaps grade school and middle school, high school that continued all the way throughout with the same group of people, a good debate coach and inspiring individual who was able to expose you to a wide variety of different ideas.

MF: Right. His name, by the way, was Noel Selegzi.

MF: Noel Selegzi.

HB: Very good. Congratulations to Mr Selegzi who clearly had an enormous impact on you and doubtless many others. So I'm getting a better sense of your early academic and social environment, but I have a couple of other questions. Were you ever interested in other academic areas? What about mathematics or science?

MF: I was never drawn to the natural sciences. I can give the autobiographical explanation and then I can try to give the philosophical justification, understanding the two. One may just be a rationalization for the other.

HB: Just give me the one that you think is true.

MF: Well, that's the whole point: there are two different questions. Again, turning to Hume, there's the question of what *is*, and there's the question of what *ought* to be.
There's the question of what is the actual psychological motivation that led me towards the humanities and away from the sciences and towards the humanistic exploration of politics.

Because of course, this is something that's very much a live question within political science and political studies: unlike something that clearly should be studied through scientific approaches, or clearly should be studied through humanistic approaches, politics—which really is a subject matter rather than a discipline—has within it a conflict between the two.

There are social scientific experimentally quantitative approaches, together with more formal mathematical approaches, like exist in economics. So you have statisticians, you have economists, you have experimenters and so forth, but then you also have philosophers. So you have the full range of humanistic and scientific approaches involved in the study of politics.

HB: I want to get to that. I want to get to that in terms of what sentimentalist approaches imply about how we move forwards in the political realm and political theory, as well as politics writ large and perhaps the social sciences more broadly.

But what I'm asking is a different question. I'm not asking to what extent politics, or social science more generally, could or should be studied from a humanities or natural sciences perspective. I'm just asking, "How come you weren't interested in physics?"

MF: Well, I was bad at physics labs.

HB: You see, *that's* the sort of answer I was expecting.

MF: I have profound respect for the subject matter. When I'm inspired by Hume's empiricism, that's not just a philosophical doctrine. I have profound respect for, and certainly enjoy reading, work by people who actually look at the way the world operates. But I'm not particularly good at that myself. I'm happy to read their work. I think I don't have the temperament for it in a certain respect. I watched Marc Hauser resign in disgrace when he was caught fabricating his monkey data.

The nice thing about a philosophical approach is you read the books you need to read, you think very hard: it's all on you. And when you sit down to do the work, you either make a good argument or a bad argument and luck doesn't have very much to do with it.

But if you're having a bad day with your monkeys and they aren't cooperating, you may not get the data that you really feel you should be getting. And in my high-school labs, I was always tempted to fudge the data because I knew that I wasn't getting the result I should be getting.

HB: Right. Some people turn into theorists, by the way, after having struggled with labs—they don't all necessarily turn into political philosophers.

MF: I lacked the mathematical skills to do theoretical physics. Certainly theoretical physicists have a kind of philosophical inclination, and I've found them often to be the natural scientists I end up getting to know best and becoming friends with the most. They very often have a real interest in philosophical topics, but they also have this mathematical ability that I just happen to lack. In a high-pressure environment that I had in high school, you learn very quickly what you're good at and what you're bad at.

HB: Were there different cliques in your high school for the science types and the humanities types?

MF: Not really. There were some people who were just fantastic at everything. For example, a friend of mine, Aaron Einbond, who now teaches at City, University of London, in the music department was just fantastic at everything. He could do physics, he could do history (he published in a peer review journal when he was still in high school), and he could write music; and that's the one he ended up pursuing. I was never one of those polymaths, but I had friends who were.

Meanwhile, I do see certain approaches to ethics and political philosophy that have a very sharp divide between the kind of a priori knowledge that they see as absolutely necessary to prevent moral principles from being contaminated by facts, while the approach that is attractive to me is so in part because I enjoy being a consumer of, not just science, but all sorts of empirical literature. Although Hume is very famous for saying, "You can't deduce an *ought* from an *is*," he still begins by looking at *what is*.

I'm not really a historian, what I do is very close to intellectual history. And often intellectual historians think I'm trying to do intellectual history and I'm doing it badly, but that's not really what I'm trying to do at all. But I love beginning from intellectual history, and working from there to do something political and philosophical.

I think literature can inform work on the moral sentiments, too, in a way that Martha Nussbaum has made very famous: her idea that philosophy—moral philosophy in particular—should often begin from literature. I don't want to say that such an approach is empirical, exactly, but it's another way of approaching these sorts of questions.

I think the right kind of approach to asking normative moral and political questions and getting answers that we can live with as human beings, isn't to *exclude*, as somehow impure or tainted, any of the different approaches. But we each have our own area of expertise: there are the things that we're competent to produce, and there are things we're merely competent to consume.

HB: Right. Looking to your family environment for a moment: was there also a sense of the importance of human inquiry through a variety of different approaches there? Was this a notion that was reinforced at home?

MF: Very much so. We had a book-filled house and both my parents were very well-educated. My mother was very much a Freudian: she was a psychoanalytic social worker—both my parents are retired now. When I studied Freud in college, I just took her collected works with me.

HB: She was okay with that?

MF: Yeah. Well, you know, if your mother loves you enough...there are all sorts of weirdnesses that come from having a Freudian mother.

But many people in my position went through exactly that. And I like talking about that whenever I lecture on Freud to this day.

HB: Was your father worried that you were going to kill him, by the way?

MF: Well, he definitely was not on the same page as my mother on this. Both are ethnically Jewish, and my father was the religious one, and she was an atheist in that distinctively Freudian way.

And I think having parents who disagreed on the big questions in life was a great example for me. You know, the primary lesson of a "great books education" is that, since the great books disagree on virtually everything, there are no unquestioned authorities because the authorities question one another. My parents, the two first authorities in my life, disagreed with one another on the big issues.

My father's Judaism was always a very philosophically informed one. The two main intellectual inspirations in his life, arguing with one another at the Jewish Theological Seminary in the generation before his, were the rationalist, pragmatist-inspired theologian Mordecai Kaplan and the mystic Abraham Joshua Heschel. He gave me both of their works from a very early age.

Mordecai Kaplan was actually in the nursing home with my great-grandmother, the Hebrew Home for the Aged in Riverdale. He was inspired by Émile Durkheim and by John Dewey; he had this view that you could have a kind of Judaism of communal solidarity without any need for supernatural theology.

Heschel, by contrast, was inspired by Hasidic mystics, and was very much about this kind of mystical experience of the divine.

And my father had books by both of them on his shelves. If you'd ask him today which one of those two he ultimately sides with, I'm not sure what he'd say. He's uncomfortable saying he's an atheist, but of course Kaplan didn't think you should say that either because in the Durkheimian tradition, "God-language" is a way that communities have to really talk about themselves rather than to talk about anything supernatural, and it's not language you should get rid of. But he insisted that I have a bar mitzvah and all of that.

And even after my bar mitzvah, I attended an after-school program at the Jewish Theological Seminary after my day at Hunter ended. So while the math geniuses I was in high school with would go take college-level math classes at Columbia, I'd go over there with them and take Hebrew and Theology and Talmud at the Jewish Theological Seminary; and I had some great teachers there.

Now that I'm in Norwich, I've joined the local progressive Jewish community, just because it's such a small community and they need every person they can get. And the idea that there's a thriving Jewish community in the place where the blood libel was invented is important to me.

But certainly, I don't see that kind of theological stuff playing a significant role in my work: the whole point of Enlightenment approaches to ethics was to get rid of the theological foundations. But at the same time, I grew up in a family and a tradition where critical thinking and reading and argument are so profoundly valued. That's one element of my father's worldview, and the other is that he's a lawyer. Going back for quite some time, most of the women in my family were social workers and most of the men in my family were lawyers. My dad was an assistant district attorney in Manhattan for 42 years.

HB: Do you ever feel like you just walked out of a Woody Allen movie or something?

MF: Well, it's all very stereotypical, extremely stereotypical. I'm realizing this for the first time now that I'm in living in England. Just on the train ride to come here I was having a phone interview with a reporter from the Norwich-based *Eastern Daily Press* to see what a New Yorker living in Norwich thinks of the upcoming American election. I think the key to understanding Trump is that he's the dark side of everything about New York—he's a very New York character, in the same way that Bernie Sanders is a very New York character.

But it's true that this was the milieu I was in until I moved here, really: everyone had these Freudian mothers and attorney fathers, and grew up in houses filled with musty paperback copies of Philip Roth that you could sneak away with.

There's a weird dynamic here, because my parents were war babies—they weren't technically baby boomers, but they're the ones who had the great acts of rebellion against their parents. Theirs was the generation that produced, in the New York Jewish community, Woody Allen and Phillip Roth. I've had a lot of British mentors over my life too, and their generation produced the Beatles and Monty Python and all that stuff—all of these sort of subversive things. And I think a lot of Gen Xers are torn about the fact that we have nothing much to rebel against.

We feel we should be rebelling, because if we're not rebelling then we're not actually obeying our parents because they believe so strongly in rebellion. And I thought this was reaching a kind of crisis: How can you have a generational identity if you don't rebel?

But then, with my millennial students, they're even more conformist than we are. So it seems that there was something very distinctive about the baby boomer generation: they were tormented and questioning everything. And the same applies in political philosophy as well.

I mean, there was this "great generation", much like the Beatles or Monty Python or Woody Allen or Phillip Roth, doing their best work in the seventies: Rawls and Nozick and Michael Walzer and Jerry Cohen, of whom Walzer is the only living survivor.

That whole generation sort of, in so many different fields, set the agenda; and so much work in political philosophy now is just boringly derivative of Rawls or Nozick or Cohen. And it's a real problem.

At one point I thought maybe I'd become a comedy writer. In comedy, in music, in philosophy, stuff done in the late sixties, seventies so utterly dominates, and we're really overdue for a rethinking of a lot of things. And it just isn't much happening in any of those fields.

HB: Well, there's still time to be a comedy writer.

MF: Well, I use it. I use it. Maybe not in my writing, but in my lectures. The best lectures have elements of stand-up comedy, and the best stand-up comedy has elements of academic lecturing.

HB: So moving on: you go to Yale for your undergraduate degree. Did you have an intellectual direction in mind from the start? You mentioned your exposure to Hume in high school—was that something you thought about pursuing in more detail at that point?

MF: It's funny you used the word direction, because I showed up at Yale to enrol in the program in Directed Studies.

HB: What are Directed Studies?

MF: Directed Studies was created after World War II, when you had all these GI bill kids coming in, who didn't have the kind of classical education that the prep school kids traditionally had—it was a way of giving them that in a year long boot camp.

And it evolved over the years. When I took it, you were required to take three set courses for your freshman year: one in philosophy—Plato to Nietzsche; one in literature—Homer to Joyce; and one in politics. It bore certain resemblances to the core curriculum at Columbia or Chicago, but unlike the core curricula it was optional. It was by application. And that meant that the students who were in it *really* wanted to be there. I know whenever I'm teaching something that's a required course, it has an atmosphere to it that is not entirely positive.

HB: Sure, you feel like an enforcer.

MF: Right, exactly. But this was different: there was a group within the incoming freshman class who really wanted to have that traditional core curriculum, great-books oriented freshman year experience. From my perspective, I really enjoyed what we did during those three weeks at American University I told you about, and I basically wanted to keep doing that.

And after a week on Kant I immediately decided, OK, sophomore year, one of the people I want to keep spending time with is Kant—so, foolishly for a sophomore, I took Alan Woods' Kant seminar, which was the most challenging academic experience I had in college.

I did an interdisciplinary major in ethics, politics, and economics. Part of what makes me not a philosopher from the point of view of a philosophy department is that I've never done the sort of non-ethical and non-political parts of philosophy.

I'm a big believer in what Jerry Schneewind called "reading entire books". So I've certainly read part one of Hume's treatise, but that's never been the part I've gotten a lot out of.

I tried to read all three of Kant's critiques, but everyone who works on Kant is either a First Critique person or a Second Critique person or a Third Critique person. And I'm definitely furthest away from the First.

And since the degree was ethics, politics and economics, and not what Oxford calls it—philosophy, politics and economics—I couldn't branch out to that major area of philosophy outside ethics and politics. So I've never had that good of a background in those, comparatively speaking.

HB: But the main point is that your interests were primarily in the overlap between ethics and politics.

MF: Yes. And that's been very consistent for a very long time.

HB: So after you finished this degree, you went off to Princeton to do graduate work. Was that something that was to some extent preordained for you? Were you already thinking about graduate school when you first started at Yale, or did it happen differently?

MF: I guess it was sort of assumed that I would always go to law school, and I was very close, but then ultimately didn't take the LSAT senior year.

HB: So, how was your dad with that?

MF: Oh, he was fine with it. Years later, when I was a postdoc at Brown, he came to one of my undergraduate lectures and said afterwards, "*Oh, that was so legalistic.*" And he meant it as a compliment.

So it's not as if law school would have been that different, and certainly if I had done that I probably would have become a legal academic. But he actually discouraged me from going to law school at some point. He asked if I want to be a lawyer, and I told him, "*No, not really.*" So he said, "*Well, then you shouldn't go to law school.*"

MF: I thought about going to Oxford or Cambridge, but at the end I decided to go to Princeton. I sometimes think about how my life would have been different, because Istvan Hont, the great scholar of Adam Smith in 18th-century political economy, would have been my advisor at Cambridge. Although I naturally have a great deal of respect for him, we have sort of diametrically opposed approaches to the material.

He is very much associated with what's called the "Cambridge school", where it's all about treating these texts as artifacts of intellectual history, and putting them in context. Whereas, what I do is all about reclaiming them for contemporary use today, which is the kind of creative anachronism that Istvan and Quentin Skinner were very much opposed to.

But I ended up going to Princeton, and studied with George Kateb until he retired. Generally speaking, I was surrounded by political theorists and philosophers in Rawls' orbit—Kateb was very much anti-Rawls, as it happened)—but generally Princeton was this place where Rawls really was setting the agenda. I mean, Rawls has his arguments for why technically speaking, political philosophy is distinct from moral philosophy. But that doesn't prevent people like Raymond Geuss from going on and on about what a terrible moralist he is. So it was all these sort of moral philosophy type approaches to political philosophy.

Questions for Discussion:

1. To what extent do you think Michael's scholarly training influences how he looks back on his own past?

2. In what ways did your high-school years impact your career? Might you have made different choices had you been exposed to other experiences?

II. Sympathy

And how to use it

HB: So let's move directly now into the core idea behind sentimentalist theory as outlined in *The Enlightenment of Sympathy*. Most people naturally associate the Enlightenment with the triumph of rationality, so the question of what sentiment has to do with Enlightenment is a fairly obvious one to pop up at the very beginning. So what are we talking about here, exactly?

MF: You can understand enlightenment in various different ways. You can understand it as a historical period—the so-called "long 18th century" written with a capital "E"—but if you want to understand it as a movement with a goal, certainly the figure who's still most important in our understanding of what enlightenment is and what its goals were, is Immanuel Kant.

Kant sort of dominated my graduate training via Rawls. There's a kind of Harvard-Princeton doctrine of Kant the father and Rawls the son—and we all want to be the third part of that Trinity, and we all fail to achieve it. So Kant defines enlightenment as us overcoming our immaturity and being able to think for ourselves. *Sapere aude*—dare to be wise—he says in his essay, "What Is Enlightenment?". That's the motto of enlightenment: dare to think for yourself.

In the book I call that "reflective autonomy": the idea of thinking for yourself, reflecting on your own preexisting moral and political commitments and coming to evaluate them, only accepting them if they can survive that process of reflection and rejecting anything that can't.

But just because you're committed to reflective autonomy doesn't mean that you're committed to any one particular theory of what that reflection should involve.

And certainly the dominant picture we have of the Enlightenment now, is one in which that reflection is reasoning. And this is very much grounded in much older images, like Platonic images of the soul, as one where reason ought to be in charge. That's identified with the *true* self; and anything else—appetites, inclinations, emotions—is not the true self.

The idea is that, as per the Kantian framework I just described, in order for us to be autonomous and self-governing, since the true self is the rational self, autonomy involves obedience to one's own reason alone; and any role for what Kant calls "inclination" in our reflection would make that reflection heteronomous, or unfree—not deriving from the self.

HB: So there is this hierarchy that is being imposed.

MF: Right: there's a sense of hierarchy within the psyche, and there's a sense that the true self is identified with only the highest member of that hierarchy, which is the rational self.

And in some ways, I'm playing a rhetorical trick here, because nowadays we all hate hierarchy and love democratic egalitarianism, and I'm especially playing a rhetorical trick, because Hume and Smith weren't democratic egalitarians in politics—I criticize Hume especially for that in the book—but in a sense, that sort of political philosophy all goes back to that original Platonic analogy between the city and the soul, between politics and psychology.

And the Kantian Enlightenment, the rationalist Enlightenment, looks like the Platonic regime: you have reason as the philosopher king, and everyone else obeys. Whereas there's a kind of democratic egalitarianism of the soul in the picture of autonomous reflection that Hume and Smith and Herder and other sentimentalists put forward.

It's still very much "dare to be wise", *sapere aude*, question everything, come to your own conclusions, think for yourself. But now that "thinking" isn't something that you do with only one element of your psychology as opposed to other elements of your psychology. It's a process by which you draw on *all* of these various faculties.

HB: So there's a sense of a synoptic process that seems to be happening in this view, insofar as its proponents are not so much denying the importance of reason and rationality—they're saying that this process of reflection incorporates that—but we also have to incorporate these other things and it's not as if these things are necessarily subservient to reason.

MF: Right. Now, admittedly there are moments when Hume sounds like he's arguing for something just as hierarchical, only flipped. He's infamous for saying that reason is, and ought only to be, the slave of the passions.

HB: And you say that that's actually taken out of context by many people, or at least represents a philosophical approach that actually shouldn't be attributed to Hume.

MF: Well, I think it's important to understand sentimentalism as a *movement* and not just as Hume and Humeanism. Hume is often a naughty boy, and he enjoys saying shocking things. And that's a very shocking thing to say.

But I think the best way to look at things—I can't remember right now who it was who first pointed this out—is that when he says reason is, and ought only to be, the slave of the passions, it's a slave almost in the sense in which Roman aristocrats had well-educated Greek slaves be the tutors to their children.

The idea is that, ultimately, reason can't set the agenda by itself. But it can educate, it can inform, it can contribute in ways that the language of it being "enslaved to the passions" can obscure.

And certain other people who I identify as sentimentalists, because they do adopt this kind of psychological holism, adopted the diametrically opposed rhetorical strategy: rather than denigrating reason, they redefine it. They try to say that *reasoning* is this certain process—Herder, for example, makes this argument—that reasoning is a process that draws on every element of human psychology. Shaftesbury says that too to a certain extent.

And really those are two different rhetorical strategies for making the same point: that when we engage in autonomous reflection, we have to draw on every resource we have at our disposal psychologically.

HB: So let's talk a little bit about what that means, exactly, because I can imagine somebody reading this thinking, *OK, I understand those who are advocating the primacy of reason, particularly at this time. After all, this follows directly in the footsteps of the great triumphs of modern science led by Galileo and Newton—there's this clear socio-historical context arguing for the benefits of taking a more dispassionate, mathematical approach to solving a wide range of problems. And there is thus a corresponding hope that some of these concepts might bear fruit when applied to more human-centric issues.*

So there is this hierarchical structure that seems to have a basis in these relatively recent great scientific discoveries, all of which also seem to argue that emotional outbursts or biases—flying of the handle and letting our passions get the better of us, say—are not only unproductive, but can often be downright counterproductive.

But then these sentimentalists come along with their holistic approach: they're not denigrating reason per se, they're not saying that we shouldn't involve rational processes, but they're saying there's more stuff going on than just reason and rationality.

And my question would then be, *Well, what **is** that, exactly? What are these other things that are going on that we should pay attention to and why are they relevant here?*

MF: Well, first off, it's true what you are saying. There was a great deal of what I would call "natural science envy". Many people worshipped Newton, recognizing that he had really accomplished something tremendous in understanding nature and they were motivated to, in turn, develop what they called "a new science of man", trying to be the Newtons of human life.

And for the sentimentalists, the key faculty—the one that plays the analogous role of gravity for Newton's theories of nature—is not "reason", but what they called "sympathy". The word empathy wasn't coined in English until the 20th century.

The idea being that, *Yes, you're right, we don't want to fly off the handle, we don't want to be out of control.* There was a sort of ancient, stoic ideal, or even Platonic ideal, of psychological harmony, psychological equilibrium—equilibrium both internally, having one's own psychology in order, and also externally, socially, achieving a kind of peace or balance between different people with conflicting interests and conflicting worldviews.

For them, the faculty that holds it all together, especially socially, isn't reason, it's sympathy. And sympathy itself is given different anatomies, different accounts of how it works. It usually can't be understood in terms of reason or emotion or imagination alone—imagination being another important faculty.

I think the best account of it is the one we find in Adam Smith, where it involves a kind of imaginative projection onto someone else's situation, working out what to feel if we were them in that situation, comparing what they're actually feeling and doing to what we would feel or do, and then trying to bring those things into equilibrium with one another.

It's the fact that we crave sympathy with one another, that there's nothing we want more than for others to sympathize with us and we want to sympathize with others: that's the glue that holds it all together, socially.

And then we internalize that, through a process of socialization and psychological maturation, and we develop what Smith calls "the impartial spectator within", whose approval and sympathy we also crave.

And we can't have internal, psychological harmony without that conscience, without that impartial spectator within, also approving of us. So both internally—psychologically—and externally—socially—what holds it all together is sympathy, not reason.

HB: So my sense is that there are two clear implications here from this approach. The first is that, if we want to understand why humans act the way they do, we shouldn't be looking to *first* apply some sort of abstract mathematical framework like what might account for how the planets move, but first simply look closely at what's actually going on.

And when you do that, what you discover is that this idea of interacting with other people, of caring for other people, of having relations with other people, is an essential part of being human. It's part of every human society that we've known. So we have to pay attention to it.

MF: Right. But you don't stop with the way we are.

HB: Right—that's the second bit. Once you recognize the way people are, you try to interpret and understand that in more detail, which brings you to this core notion of sympathy and equilibrium and all of that. Is that a fair summary?

MF: Right—so you begin with the way human beings are. And you understand, unlike with certain attempts to get a view from nowhere, that we don't have any resources outside of ourselves for moving from figuring out how things are to evaluating how they should be.

But we *can* see whether or not what we're currently doing can bear reflective scrutiny. We use all the resources at our disposal to turn them on ourselves and ask whether or not we can bear the test of full knowledge of what we're doing and what motivates us to do it.

This is in contrast to the sort of a priori, fully rationalist approach to ethics, which asks, *What moral rules are incumbent on any rational being as such?*

And later, Schopenhauer makes fun of Kant, saying, *Why are you so concerned about rational beings **as such**? The only rational beings we know are human beings. You must be weeping over the dear little angels, the non-human rational beings that you're worried you're somehow discriminating against, by beginning an investigation of ethics with an investigation of human nature.*

And those who reject that a priori approach do what David Miller recently called "political philosophy for Earthlings"—being focused on what kind of ethical and social and political life can work for beings like *us*, because those are the only kind of rational beings we know.

And it just so happens, the only kind of rational beings we know aren't *merely* rational beings: they have all these other things in common with one another that can be the basis of a shared moral and political life, and they don't have all that much to do with their rationality as such.

Which is not to say that rationality *isn't* one of the things that all the beings we're concerned with have in common. It is. And if somehow you have an ethical system grounded in rational errors, irrationalities, that would be a problem. But it's not the *only* resource we have available for human beings.

HB: You describe how one of the things that Hume does, when he tries to give a more concrete characterization of this notion of sympathy, is to urge us to deliberately invoke a broader perspective in order to transcend our own biases. Our reflective capacity should therefore include asking things like, "*How do things look from this objective third party?*"

MF: The metaphor he uses is how we determine the size of material objects through multi-perspectival thinking. So, as we move about the world, we know that objects don't shrink and grow as we move further away from or closer to them. We develop this kind of instinctive ability to look at things from a general point of view, to think about how they look from a variety of perspectives, from a single meta-perspective that takes into account all these different angles—a general point of view on things.

And the way instinctual sympathies work, *before* they go through this process of reflective correction, is that someone else's joy or sorrow—very much like a physical object—seems greater the closer you are to them—closer in *all* senses of the word: being in close physical proximity to someone experiencing an emotion, having a strong, personal familial or even national connection—all of those reasons why you might describe yourself as being "close to someone".

And as you go through the world, and you move closer to and further away from various people, you have to understand that their subjective experiences and emotions don't grow and shrink as you move closer to or further away from them any more than physical objects do.

So you have to develop what Hume calls "a general point of view" and what Smith refers to as "an impartial spectator".

David Foster Wallace has some fantastic stuff on this. He thought that this is what literature is all about: that every human being is the centre of his or her own universe and our natural tendency is to become self-involved in our own experience of the world, extended slightly by a small community that we're close to, and we only see things from *their* point of view.

Ancient stoicism was a very important influence on everyone during this period, both rationalist and sentimentalist. But in this respect the sentimentalists, with their idea of an impartial spectator or general point of view, are drawing on the ancient stoic image of the expanding circle: that you can begin with yourself, expand it out to family, expand it out to community, expand it out to country; and then eventually the stoic ideal is one of cosmopolitanism in the original sense of being a citizen of the universe.

There's a great book by Fonna Forman-Barzilai on Adam Smith and the expanding circle (*Adam Smith and the Circles of Sympathy*). The idea is that the progress of sentiments—the process of psychological maturation and development and reflective improvement that Hume and Smith and Herder and Hutcheson and Shaftesbury describe—is best understood as a combination of the Newtonian quasi-scientific attempt to describe the world as it actually is and the ancient stoic conception, revived by Wittgenstein, of philosophy as therapy.

Perhaps this is my Freudian mother's influence, but the idea is that the goal is not simply "knowledge of truth via reason", but rather a process of becoming a responsible, emotionally mature adult human being by expanding beyond the infantile narcissism that you see in toddlers or Donald Trump or people with unacceptable levels of moral and political immaturity, and expanding that out to reach a general understanding via emotionally mature, moral sentiments. So it's a kind of scientifically informed therapeutic process rather than pure psychological science.

Questions for Discussion:

1. To what extent do you think the "multi-perspectival thinking" that Michael describes can be taught, as opposed to being innate?

2. How certain can we be that "reason" and "sympathy" are, in fact, entirely different things?

III. Different Tracks

Hume, Smith and Herder

HB: I'd like to focus now on some of the differences between these thinkers, in particular some differences between David Hume and Adam Smith.

I'll begin by saying that my sense is that any empirical approach to investigating human society seems to have a naturally conservative tendency associated with it. So, for example, supposing you are interested in examining the way people have interacted with each other in the past in order to develop a theory of justice. And you might naturally be tempted to say something like, "*Society is structured in such a way that there is this particular type of interaction between these individuals that is generally perceived to be in the public good, and that seems to be working.*"

And that might lead you to conclude that there's not much we should do to rock the boat—hence the conservatism. And my understanding is that your view of Hume involves this very concern: that you think there's a bit of a problem here with his notion of justice that does arise from this sense of conservatism. And to some extent you feel that it is corrected by Smith. So my first question is: Is that a reasonably fair summary?

MF: Yes.

HB: OK. My second question is, Well, how should we deal with all of that? What would you recommend, exactly?

MF: Right. So like any great thinker, to paraphrase Whitman, Hume contains multitudes. And it's particularly striking that, as Sheldon

Wolin the political theorist observed, Hume has the scandal of his intellectual children correlating with one another.

Hume was a direct inspiration, as I see it, to three deeply opposing philosophies and philosophers. He was a direct inspiration to Bentham and his utilitarian radicalism, who said reading Hume made the scales fall from his eyes. He was a direct inspiration to Burke, with his conservatism. And he was a direct inspiration to Smith, with his liberalism.

Hume, himself, incorporates elements of all three, with a "utilitarian conservatism" in a sense—a proto-utilitarian proto-conservatism, since those words weren't in circulation at the time.

The idea being that we have this sympathetic concern for other human beings for the reasons we were talking about before, that can be seen by our abiding by certain conventions, abiding by these tacitly agreed upon societal rules. They are not literally agreed upon in a social contract but tacitly arrived at—the metaphor he uses is the way people rowing a boat row in unison without having a cox or someone deliberately charged with coordinating them.

And these conventions are extremely important for keeping society functioning; were they to fall apart, we would have profound human suffering. So he calls it a kind of "sympathy with the public interest" that leads us to approve of obedience to the reigning conventions in any given time and place.

And he *defines* justice as the virtue of obedience to those conventions. The just person is the person who follows the conventions of property, of law—the conventional social and political practices prevalent in any given time.

So Bentham looks at that and goes, *Aha, do whatever is useful. But, Hume, you may be wrong that the conventions are the most useful thing at any given time. Maybe we should be radical and start from the ground up and try to figure out what's the most useful thing to do.*

Burke looks at that and goes, *Well. Why are you undermining these sacred conventions by saying they're merely useful? This sort of pious adoration we have of them is, in fact, **undermined** by thinking the way Hume does. So we should discourage reflection, or at least* *excessive reflection, on the utility of the conventions lest we undermine the fidelity to the conventions themselves.*

Smith, though, builds a theory of justice grounded not in a sort of aggregate sympathy with the public interest as a whole, but with—in his famously liberal, individualist, way—with our sympathy with the resentments of given individuals: that what is unjust is what injures people in ways that they can properly resent.

That when an individual has something done to them that doesn't just merely hurt them—that's not sufficient for injury in this legal sense—but that someone has done something to them that they properly resent.

To determine if this has occurred, we must imaginatively enter into the position of each of them and try to impartially judge what has happened. Has a genuine injury occurred? Or is this just an unwarranted accusation of injury?

And we have this divided sympathy, whereby we feel our way into the position of the alleged perpetrator and ask whether or not what he did was justified, and we also feel our way into the position of the alleged victim and we ask whether or not the resentment that she's feeling is justified.

And we try to bring these together and reconcile them, trying to determine, using every imaginative and emotional and rational faculty at our disposal, whether or not an injustice has actually occurred.

HB: In many ways this is what we would now call empathy.

MF: Right. Smith knows that he's stretching the meaning of what could then be called "sympathy". He begins his book on this, *The Theory of Moral Sentiments*, by saying, effectively, *You'll have to excuse me: sympathy usually just means feeling sorry for someone when they feel bad; I'm not sure I have the right word for it, but I'm going to call this thing I'm talking about "sympathy".*

By the 20th century, it more or less lines up with what we now call "empathy": this kind of imaginative projection to work out what's going on in someone else's situation. But not only that: to judge what *ought* to be going on in that situation.

Too often we think if you empathize with someone you necessarily approve of them: to understand all is to forgive all. And Smith says that it's quite the opposite. That you need to empathetically project yourself into someone's situation *in order to judge them*, in order to work out what is to be done in that situation.

And then once you work out what's to be done in that situation, you compare what *you* would do in that situation, what you feel should be done in that situation, with what that person is *actually doing*.

And if they're doing the wrong thing, then you judge them negatively—not despite, but *because* of the fact that you've empathized with them, so empathy (or what he called sympathy) is the primary faculty necessary for adequate moral judgement.

So when it comes to judgements of justice and injustice, you divide things up between two conflicting parties and work out the degree to which each is justified in his or her attitudes towards the other. And then you inductively derive general rules of justice and injustice from lots of individual examples of people injuring or not injuring, wronging or not wronging one another.

And the skills required for good judgement, for making those judgements to begin with, is sympathy—or what we would typically now call empathy.

It's interesting: there was actually a controversy a number of years ago when Barack Obama was asked, "*What is the main quality you look for in a Supreme court justice?*" and he replied, "*Empathy.*"

Well, many people were horrified by this, thinking that he was recommending that you shouldn't follow the law but simply...

HB: "Going with your gut."

MF: Right: going with your gut. In fact, a right-wing friend of mine joked that I should call my book *Basic Instinct*—that it's all just about doing what you feel.

And that's **exactly the opposite** of what I'm talking about here. It's **not** about going with your first immediate instinct, which may be biased strongly, usually biased strongly in your own favour because you haven't expanded that circle, but maybe biased for, or against, one of the parties in a dispute that you're asked to judge. You may be a spectator, but you're not an impartial spectator, because you follow this immediate inclination of exhibiting your affinity to one party in the dispute versus another.

But a process of real projective empathy, on the other hand...

HB: Involves this reflective capacity.

MF: Exactly. It's a reflective capacity that makes you a competent judge of others, as well as someone able to live at peace with your yourself.

HB: So there's another point you bring in your book that I'd like you to comment on.

It's all very well and good to be empirical and look to see what has worked in the past, and use our reflective capacity of empathy to make judgements and then build up some general rules by induction, but there is always the danger that we miss something important due to our own cultural biases: that these capacities are somehow limited or inhibited because we haven't been exposed to the full range of human possibilities given the naturally reinforcing nature of societal traditions and so forth—which brings us to this Johann Gottfried Herder fellow you mentioned earlier.

MF: Right. Herder is a very interesting figure. On the whole, I don't think he gets his due, he doesn't get a fair shake in contemporary philosophical discussions, in part because no one knows quite what to do with him.

HB: He was a student of Kant, right?

MF: Right. He was a student of "the pre-critical Kant". And that's something that really needs to be stressed. There's this cultural connection at the time with Kant where about half of his friends were Scottish: there was this sort of Königsberg-Edinburgh intellectual trade route, where Scottish ideas and Königsbergian ideas were mixing with one another.

And the pre-critical Kant—Kant before he had his midlife crisis at the age of 40—was very much a part of that. His lectures were typically advertised like, *Dr. Kant will be lecturing on the moral systems of Francis Hutcheson and Bishop Butler* (or other British sentimentalists) *and will be perfecting their moral system in his lectures.*

Herder was a student of Kant during this time, and his notes on Kant's ethics lectures are one of our best records of them. But then he very much broke with Kant after Kant turned critical and rationalist.

I have some speculations that around the age of 40, when a friend died and he realized that he would never truly achieve romantic love, Kant's heart withered away and he became the Kant we know and loathe today.

And Herder was very angry at him when that happened. He broke with Kant and picked up and ran with various ideas, especially Smith's idea of sympathy as this imaginative projection.

The story of Herder has been complicated by several things. There was an unpleasant interlude when he was embraced by various nationalists, most conspicuously the Nazis in the 20th century, because he had this idea of a kind of folk spirit.

HB: Well, the Nazis falsely appropriated a whole lot of thinkers who couldn't defend themselves because they were long dead.

MF: That's right. So Herder had this idea that there are these different "folk groups". He had a big influence on the brothers Grimm: the notion that you should go out and collect folk stories and learn about popular traditions and modes of thought, because there's some sort of popular spirit that gives each nation its distinct character.

And that *can* be given a kind of grimly Teutonic spin: we're going to collect the folk ways of our people and celebrate those. But Herder himself was not a cosmopolitan of imperial uniformity—he was a great critic of imperialism—but had a cosmopolitanism of appreciating the very different worldviews and folk ways of lots of different national and cultural groups. So he's one of the key figures.

There are a couple of things he *almost* does, but doesn't quite do. He almost starts using the word culture in the plural—*Kulturen*.Up until Herder, there was this idea that there was *one* path of human culture and cultivation, and either you were cultured or you weren't.

Herder says, *No. Cultivation culture is this multi-branched forking pathway that can go in all sorts of different directions.* He didn't quite make the grammatical step of literally pluralizing the term culture— he didn't say *Kulturen*—but the ideas are all there.

The same is true of *Einfühlung*, the German term that in the mid-twentieth century was translated as empathy. He says, *The way you feel your way into all of these different cultural possibilities is through something like these processes of imaginative projection that Smith describes on the individual level.*

So Herder was very concerned with collecting and translating the literatures of all sorts of different cultures. He was a Lutheran pastor but he was very adamant in his scriptural hermeneutics in pointing out that, to 18th and 19th-century Prussians, these are the writings of a very distant and very foreign literature and worldview and culture that you have to "feel your way into".

And he keeps saying, "*Feel your way into this; feel your way into that.*"

And this sense of feeling your way into—*Einfühlung* is the German term that was picked up—became a huge influence on Romanticism. A prominent theme is this idea of a kind of aesthetic experience of feeling your way into a work of art, either a work of art from an idiosyncratic individual genius—which is what the Romantics were all obsessed with—or in Herder's multicultural version, a work of art of a people, perhaps a piece of folk art, but from a folk very different from one's own, where the aesthetic experience is all about this imaginative projection.

So this enters into the mainstream of German Romantic aesthetics. In early 20th-century, English translations of late 19th-century German aesthetics is the first time you see the German *Einfühlung* being translated into empathy. And that's a story that traces back to Herder, although he never actually uses the word *Einfühlung,* just as he never uses the word *Kulturen.*

But what that means is that he uses, specifically Smith's, but more generally these anglophone ideas of the moral sentiments. He's one of the pathways by which that becomes romanticized and enters into the story of German Romanticism, which isn't a story I pursue—that's not a path that is particularly useful to me—but there's a real relevance between his approach and some contemporary issues.

Today we are *obsessed* with issues of cultural identity and multiculturalism, and while much of the Enlightenment is castigated as racist and sexist and imperialist and xenophobic—and Hume and Smith themselves are hardly the greatest people when it comes to considering the import of human diversity for their theories—but Herder is.

Herder really is among the first people to grapple with the full implications of the complete spectrum of human diversity in all times and places. And he adapts the moral sentimentalist theory in a way to deal with this fact of human diversity, in a way that strikes me as very unique.

I'm not sure. I mean, Enlightenment rationalism is constantly being accused of being the ideology of western imperialism, and Kant certainly does have horrible things to say about non-European peoples.

Hume isn't great on human pluralism. He's okay. He's not as bad as some from that era. But he does tend to think that there's one correct way of doing things. Even if it's one that's not arrived at through reason alone, there is more or less one best way.

The thing is it's often someone else's way rather than ours on some particular issue. So, for example, Hume thinks that there's no plausible justification for the abhorrence to suicide in the Christian West. He thinks that the ancient stoics and the modern Japanese who don't think suicide is morally prohibited—indeed there may be some circumstances where it's morally required of us—he thinks they get it right and we get it wrong.

So, even if you're a monist—you believe there's one true way—you could justify your monism in different ways. You could be a monist for rationalist reasons, you could be a monist for sentimentalist reasons.

Sentimentalism doesn't necessarily include a pluralism. I don't want to say that it just comes automatically with the territory, it doesn't.

But even if you're a monist, the most thoroughgoing monist—*there's one and only one true way*—it doesn't necessarily imply that you are a cultural imperialist. You could think that, at least in some specific instances, say, 16th-century samurai were the ones leading the one true way, or you could be a kind of vulgar Rousseauist and say, "*Primitive humanity was leading the one best kind of life.*"

Or, for that matter, you could say, "*The one true way is some sort of hybrid that hasn't yet been fully instantiated anywhere—we can see a bit of the truth here and a bit over there.*"

So, I don't want to say all monists are necessarily imperialists, and I don't want to say all monists are necessarily rational. So, those are two steps that absolve rationalism from the charge of *necessarily* being imperialist bastards.

But that said, in the 18th century, multiculturalism was being invented by Herder. It wasn't being invented in a rationalist way.

Maybe there are rationalist defenses of multiculturalism, but I think the best way that we actually *experience* the value of diverse ways of life is through an imaginative emotional projection into them.

That's a lot of what a good multicultural humanist education is about. It's about reading widely, about the experiences of people in all sorts of times and places, and feeling your way into their lives: expanding your circle in a distinctively empathy-based rather than reason-based way.

Without that power of imaginative empathetic projection, it would be very, very difficult, if not impossible, for us to see the value of diversity of ways of life in the way that Herder does.

Questions for Discussion:

1. Might there be some cultures that we are simply unable to "feel our way into"? If so, why might that be, exactly?

2. Are you surprised at the notion of Adam Smith, typically invoked as "the father of economics", as being so preoccupied with understanding how we should make moral judgements? How do you think this relates, if at all, to Smith's views on politics and economics?

IV. Disciplinary Boundaries

Political philosophy as Kurdistan

HB: Let me move to a bit of a sociological issue now. My understanding is that *The Enlightenment of Sympathy* grew out of your PhD work.

You've been thinking, and writing, and talking, about the importance of sentimentalism and sympathy for some time now, not only as an important strand of Enlightenment thought, but also because of its implications for the present day—a topic I hope to get to shortly.

Are you an outlier? What's the reaction that you typically face from your academic colleagues? Is it, "*That's Michael—he keeps banging on about sympathy and empathy and we humour him.*"? Or is there a growing sense that people are saying, "*This is an important part of the Enlightenment story that we need to pay more attention to.*"?

MF: The main reason I sometimes feel ill at ease in the academic world, and academic discussions of this stuff, is not because anyone thinks that any particular substantive claim I'm making is crazy, but rather because the contemporary academic world is so divided into different disciplinary silos, that making these points doesn't easily fit into any one of them.

I mentioned earlier that, intellectual historians often think, *Well, he's not a very good intellectual historian. We already know that Hume believed these things, that Smith believed these things. We're not learning anything new about intellectual history that we didn't already know.*

There are people who work on psychology, who are often reinventing the wheel and think they're discovering for the first time, the importance of theses about affect and empathy that Hume and Smith were talking about hundreds of years ago. And I'll hand them my book and they'll say, "*Yeah, we've had some experimental evidence about this. It's interesting that there were these historical precedents.*"

Then I'll hand it to a philosopher. Generally speaking, philosophy is done ahistorically: it's all about formulating arguments and evaluating them without considering whether or not they've already been made, or what the relevance of old texts might be. And many of the claims I'm making, depend for their plausibility on empirical claims about human psychology that aren't part of the repertoire of philosophical argument today.

So insofar as I've run into difficulties, it's not been because, what I'm saying seems wrong to people so much, as it doesn't fit well within the domain of any one discipline.

This is why, I suppose, I'm a political theorist, why I'm in the "discipline of politics", which is really not a discipline at all. I've often compared political philosophy to Kurdistan. We don't have actually an independent discipline of our own.

HB: But it's there.

MF: It's there. And it's divided into three—just like the Turkish, Syrian, and Iraqi segments—there's philosophy, there's history and there's politics.

The reason that I'm in politics is probably because—it most closely resembles Iraqi Kurdistan—we have our own autonomous region as political theorists, and we can more or less do our own thing; and we can welcome in and talk to our colleagues in philosophy and in history.

But these things happen. Intellectual historians suffered terribly in the discipline of history, where cultural, and social historians kept telling them, "*Why are you studying these elite texts? This isn't real history, real history is the lives of peasants!*"

In philosophy, political philosophy is often marginalized: "*Why aren't you doing analytic metaphysics and epistemology; mind your P's and Q's.*" That's what contemporary Anglophone philosophy is. So they have various Turkish-type and Syrian-type sufferings.

By contrast, we're doing pretty well in political theory.

But of course, the situation is even worse for me, because my interests are a bit broader than most. Many, many political theorists are interested in intellectual history and in philosophy. I'm also profoundly interested in psychology and sociology, and a whole lot of other stuff, like literature.

I have a piece that's coming out on how sentimentalism was interdisciplinary before the disciplines: that Hume and Smith and Herder had a general program for the study of humanity as such that cuts across everything that is today the humanities and the social sciences. And as such, it is difficult to appreciate in an age of *extreme* academic specialization.

I've seen this happen to all sorts of people, not just my own work. What starts to happen is that people don't even have to bother making the argument that something is wrong, or even that it is uninteresting or unimportant.

Instead, you make the argument in a sociology department, *This isn't really sociology*; in a philosophy department you make the argument, *This isn't really philosophy*; in a history department you make the argument, *This isn't really history*.

"*It's great*," they might say, "*but it isn't really sociology or philosophy or history*," or whatever. And if that is accepted as a valid objection to interesting work, then we have a problem.

University administrators like talking about interdisciplinarity a great deal. But as long as the professional incentives to strongly disciplinary specialization are there, we're going to face real difficulty in understanding the full extent to which work from times and places that don't share our current disciplinary boundaries, can improve our thinking.

HB: It's interesting, because as you were speaking about disciplinary boundaries, two examples popped into my head of people firmly ensconced in their discipline who said things that, to me at least, resonated quite strongly with things you have said today.

The first is Onora O'Neill, the renowned Kantian scholar, whom nobody would deny belongs in a philosophy department. I had the opportunity to talk to her recently for Ideas Roadshow.

One of her claims is that this notion of Kantian autonomy, which people talk about a lot, isn't so much the autonomy of the perfectly rational well-structured individual Prussian living in a room somewhere, but she talks about "*the autonomy of reason*" rather than "*the autonomy of the reasoners*".

Her view seems to be that an important aspect of what reason is for Kant necessarily involves some amount of social interaction and interchange.

"*That's why*", she maintains, "*When Kant talks about reason and the autonomy of reason and the moral law, he will often will invoke political and cultural arguments.*"

So for her, there is an aspect of universalism: since people sitting together in a room engaged in some dialogue can be engaged in a constructive act because the principles that they are using and advocating could be applied to any one of them, and hence there is this sense of universality.

Now, to me, as a non-philosopher, there seem to be very strong parallels with this idea and what you were saying. I mean, forget for the moment about particular words like "sympathy" or "empathy" or "justice" or "sentimentalism" or "rationality" or whatever—both of you are, it seems to me, discussing key aspects of the process, the necessary process, of how human beings must engage with one another on a societal level to make genuine progress.

So when I hear you say that someone like her is in this well-defined position over here that is so structurally distinct from where you are, that strikes me as curious. It doesn't strike me as quite different at all in many ways.

MF: Well, they're both, broadly speaking, liberal, universal, cosmopolitan, Enlightenment views—unlike an argument on the applied level between, say, a social democracy liberal and a libertarian.

On this foundational level, that commitment to Enlightenment values is shared. The question is, *How do we get there and why are we committed to that?* It's not, *What are we committed to?* It's taking a step back and asking how and why. The metaphor, in a slightly different context that the philosopher Derek Parfit has used, is, *Different paths up the same mountain.*

I have a very different kind of argument with people, whether of the left or right, who reject Enlightenment values, who don't seek to transcend the particular perspective of an individual identity group—be it an oppressed minority identity group or an aggrieved majority identity group—and who think there's some sort of epistemological privilege in a particular group membership, who reject the Enlightenment ideal of, *Thinking for yourself but at the same time, thinking in a way that incorporates the importance of the perspective of other people.*

I have a different kind of argument with opponents of liberal democracy and liberal individualism, because I do reject this thoroughgoing monism of a non-multicultural approach to ethics and politics. I'm looking for ways in which cultures can be in dialogue with one another and contribute to one another's moral development, as opposed to isolating themselves from one another.

With someone committed to a Kantian rationalist version of Enlightenment liberalism, the dispute is of a very different nature than it is with someone committed to a postmodern or a premodern form of identitarian, anti-liberal ethics or politics.

HB: OK, but my point wasn't so much saying that you were in wholesale agreement with Onora O'Neill—clearly you aren't—or that you are closer to her position than many others—clearly you are—but more that it seems to me that you are both, in your separate ways, doing many similar things and thus I am quite bemused by the notion that there is some sort of disciplinary wall between you.

Let me move on to my second example along the same lines. You've contrasted, both today and in your book, what you are doing with intellectual history. You explicitly said, "*I'm not doing intellectual history,*" and you talked about how you're more interested in reclaiming past ideas for contemporary use rather than simply examining them on their own terms, as opposed to people like Istvan Hont and Quentin Skinner from "the Cambridge School".

But here, you see, I got bemused again. Let me tell you why. I've also had the very good fortune to have an Ideas Roadshow conversation with Quentin Skinner, where we talked about his neo-Roman view of freedom (*Quest For Freedom*). The details of that aren't terribly relevant, but what did strike me as quite relevant was his very clear exposition of his motivations for conducting research in the first place.

He said, "*History is written by the winners, but a key question for me is, Did the winners always deserve to win?*" He went on to explain that rather than engaging in historical inquiry to account for where we are today, he was generally much more interested in examining past ideas and concepts to evaluate to what extent meritorious ideas that have been somehow discarded might be brought back to light— he used the metaphor of looking for buried treasure.

So when I hear you say something like, "*Look, there are aspects of these ideas of moral sentimentalism that people like Hume and Smith and Herder were really big on which have been, if not wholly ignored, at least significantly overlooked,*" that doesn't strike me as terribly different, in spirit, to what seems to be driving someone who is generally acknowledged to be one of the greatest intellectual historians of our time. So once again, I'm confused.

MF: Right. I actually have a piece on this that I'm trying to get published right now ("The Ethics of Interpretation in Political Theory and Intellectual History," *The Review of Politics*, December 2019). I take solace from the fact that Quentin himself points out that his sort of great programmatic statement from early in his career, his essay, "Meaning and Understanding and the History of Ideas", was rejected from something like 30 journals before it was accepted somewhere. And I'm going through a similar experience with an article about him.

And the argument I make there—and I can see why in a world where so many of his students control so many journals, I'm having trouble getting this published—is that what he preached early in his career isn't what his most valuable contribution to actual scholarly practice is.

When he was attacking people like Leo Strauss and John Plamenatz for their kind of "text worship" and was arguing that historical texts need to be read in the context of their time, he wasn't at that time doing what he did in later decades, which was to look for these buried treasures in the past, evaluate them on their merits and see if they could be useful to us today.

Again, this is another example of the baby boom generation doing the sort of path-setting work in the sixties and seventies that we're still struggling with today. There were statements like John Dunn's work on Locke saying, "*Locke can't be understood independent of his distinctive theological context, and since he's so thoroughly theological in that distinctive 17th-century way, he's of no use to us now in thinking through political matters.*"

You had a lot of this kind of critical destructive contextualism going on, and you had these programmatic essays, these methodological essays coming out of Cambridge that were all about how political philosophy is over here, intellectual history is over there; and the main task of intellectual history is putting the past in the past where it belongs.

If you want to do political philosophy, as Quentin Skinner said in that "Meaning and Understanding "essay, you have to do your thinking for yourself, you can't rely on the past.

And although he republished his early programmatic essays, his methodological essays, in 2002, I believe, he never said, "*I'm doing this different other project now.*"

I think his whole attempt to find alternatives in the past, specifically his theory of neo-Roman liberty, but there are other examples that he and his circle have been working on, isn't really a "purely historical" project, in that sense of history being *strictly* "knowledge of the past" that most of the time just ends up showing its irrelevance for the present.

It is, in contrast, a political theoretical, political philosophical project, but it's rarely forthrightly declared as being that. I mean, it's odd to say that when you tell me that to you he was just straight-forwardly telling you, "*This is what I'm doing.*"

It's funny. Marx famously complained, "*I'm not a Marxist.*" Maybe Skinner—together with many of the best figures coming out of Cambridge like Pocock and Dunn and Hont—maybe at their best they never really were "Cambridge School historians".

Ultimately though, when it comes to the subject of disciplinary boundaries, unlike the example you were giving before—where I really *do* think there's a substantive disagreement with the Rawls' neo-Kantian project that was carried on by his students in various ways, like Christine Korsgaard, and Onora O'Neill—if we all agree that we should be reading old books and trying to use them to figure out how we can solve our moral and political problems now, then there is no disagreement.

But I don't think there's any denying that the methodological work that Skinner did early in his career set up a self-image of what counts as "real history" and what doesn't.

And if you buy that image—and he may not; these sort of things take on a life of their own, and whether or not, biographically, the originator still believes in them is a wholly separate question—but if you believe in a vision that, "*History is just about the past; and if you're talking about the present, then you're not doing history,*" then I'm happy to say, "*I'm not doing history. I'm doing political philosophy or political theory or something like that.*"

Of course, then the philosophers will start saying, "*Well, if you're not doing X, Y, and Z, you're not doing philosophy.*" And then I'll just say, "*Okay, fine. Then I'm not doing philosophy either.*"

Because of the way the bureaucracy of disciplinary divisions works, these disciplinary labels can play an important rhetorical role in many academic arguments, but I think ultimately they're intellectually unhelpful.

Questions for Discussion:

1. To what extent is it possible to be doing truly innovative work within an established, very well-defined, discipline?

2. Why do you think so many academic administrators talk about the merits of "interdisciplinarity"? What sorts of things do they have in mind, exactly, and what is their agenda for doing so?

V. Bringing It Home

Moral sentiments in the real world

HB: Let's move to the implications of your work for the present day, which is clearly something that you're passionate about. Let's begin by first looking within the academic realm. We've talked a little bit about this already, with our discussion of disciplinary silos and so forth.

But let's now just look within those disciplines themselves to see where possible impact might lie. As you've already mentioned, we have fields like social science and neuroscience. Of course there's economics too, but I'm always loath to regard that as an actual academic discipline, which is one of the reasons that I've never actually spoken to an economist for Ideas Roadshow.

MF: Well, you may want to, because I think what's going on in economics right now reflects something that I think my work is a part of. We're seeing the rise of various forms of psychological approaches in various social sciences, in economics it's called behavioural economics, and its done experimentally. There are various strengths and weaknesses of that. But the basic insight that human beings are not pure rational beings is one that's now being appreciated in distinctive ways—

HB: Well, that's nice. But given that it's taken them the better part of 100 years to formally recognize what anyone who's ever lived on planet Earth for five years or so is trivially aware of, you'll excuse my lack of enthusiasm at their recent epiphany.

It's hard to think of a better example of how theoretical assumptions could be so overwhelmingly wrong for so overwhelmingly long than "classical economic theory" with its silly maximization of utility functions.

MF: In their defense, Milton Friedman had this famous essay where he pointed out that, "These economic models were never meant to capture reality as it actually is. That they were supposed to function...."

HB: Well, they *don't* function.

MF: Right. That's the problem.

HB: Well, how *could* they possibly function? They're completely wrong. Their assumptions have no ontological value whatsoever. I mean, how could I expect a model of disease transmission based on, say, analyzing discarded banana peels to actually function?

   Look, I should be clear. I'm not saying that economics is irrelevant. It is, of course, *hugely* relevant. Questions about social inequality and how to best set fiscal and monetary policy are obviously tremendously important to vast numbers of people. But that's very different than economics as an academic discipline, in my mind.

MF: Right.

HB: That's the distinction that I'm making here. I'm certainly not saying that decisions made by finance departments or the Federal Reserve or the IMF or the World Bank don't have an impact on people. Of course they have an enormous impact.

MF: It is striking that in this whole conversation, we haven't once mentioned that Adam Smith did write this other book too: *The Wealth of Nations*.

HB: Yeah.

MF: Which I don't claim to have any particular expertise in. I mean, I've taught it, and I don't think there's an "Adam Smith" problem. I think he's very clear in *The Theory of Moral Sentiments*—and this has been so relevant lately—that you should understand the pursuit of wealth as grounded in a kind of easily understandable mistake, that is common to toddlers and Donald Trump, that really what people most crave from their fellow human beings is sympathetic concern and approval.

One way not to get that is to be observed and disapproved of, but another way not to get that is to be ignored entirely—not to be paid attention to. The thing about wealth is that it's a very good way to get people to pay attention to you.

The ideal of human life *should* be paid attention to because of one's worthy accomplishments. But we do have an unfortunate tendency to ignore the poor and to pay attention to the wealthy, and there are some wealthy and prominent people whom we admire. There are other wealthy and prominent people we pay attention to and disapprove of, but like a toddler throwing a temper tantrum who wants you to pay attention to him and doesn't care whether you do so with approval or disapproval, a certain kind of pursuit of wealth, or self-interest comes from this desire to be acknowledged and paid attention to.

It comes from a kind of misplaced version of the same principles, which if taken in a slightly different direction would actually make you a genuinely admirable person. But because they go wrong in this very psychologically understandable way, they lead to a single-minded pursuit of self-interest.

And Smith, in *The Wealth of Nations*, makes the further point that—and this is something that a lot of people who work on *The Wealth of Nations* have paid a lot of attention to—so many of us *do* pursue material things very single-mindedly. The assumption we do so *rationally* as opposed to making lots of mistakes in our pursuit of them may be wrong, but the basic assumption that human beings are self-interested isn't off the mark.

You can *rely* on someone's self-interest, but being self-interested in that way doesn't actually make us happy, but we do it anyway. And in a kind of deist way, Smith can say that this error as to how to pursue our individual happiness has, because of the workings of the market, all of these remarkably positive unintended consequences for economic growth as a whole.

And that economic growth does a lot to alleviate poverty—and Smith is always concerned primarily with the alleviation of poverty, because poverty really *is* a threat to human happiness.

But once you've escaped poverty—and today's empirical psychologists and sociologists and behavioural economists try to figure out approximately where this line is—you reach a point where the further pursuit of wealth beyond that point doesn't actually do anything to make you happy anymore.

The consistency of all of that in Smith's writings is the assumption of self-interest that gets the economics going. And *The Wealth of Nations* is explained in *The Theory of Moral Sentiments* as a *misfiring*, albeit a very, very common one, of the same psychological forces responsible for our most laudable moral propensities.

HB: What do you think Adam Smith would say now if we could resurrect him and show him contemporary American and British society?

MF: I've seen some very good work on the extent to which it's a mistake to identify the contemporary economic system with what he was advocating. It's important to remember that Smith was an opponent of the early versions of what we would now call "the multinational corporation".

He didn't think something like the East India company with its drive towards a monopoly, with its separation of ownership and management, with its sheer size, was something that should be a feature of a healthy free market.

My work isn't about Smith's economics. I'm not sure, I have no worked-out theory, as to whether or not a genuinely free market,or what Smith calls "the system of natural liberty", really is the best economic system.

But even if it is, it shouldn't be identified, in any way, really, with the economic status quo. The economic status quo, I think, is all about close government enmeshment with giant corporations of a sort that bears very little resemblance to what Smith would see as "markets".

Deborah Boucoyannis has a great paper on this ("The Equalizing Hand: Why Adam Smith Thought the Market Should Produce Wealth Without Steep Inequality"): the emergence of inequality, significant inequality, the emergence of high rates of profit, which is something that economists today are happy to acknowledge, are all signs that there *isn't* actually market competition going on.

So a situation where you have growing inequality, growing consolidation of capital in larger and larger corporations, isn't one we should identify with the economic system that Smith advocated.

Now that said, in the book, I do say that, although I'm endorsing a lot of Hume's ideas, his conservative political philosophy can be rejected on Humean grounds. I think it's a whole separate issue to ask, *Can we argue with Smith against Smith when it comes to his economic vision?*

HB: Sure, but the reason I'm asking isn't so much to be trying to cherry pick particular aspects of Smith's economic framework, but rather to simply point out that Adam Smith the man, was a moralist: he was first and foremost interested in the moral development of human societies and the human condition.

MF: Right.

HB: Now, he believed that there were particular economic pathways that would best achieve a moral end, and one can argue whether they were successful or unsuccessful. But my understanding is that they were means to an end, and they were important means to an end concerning suffering, inequality, poverty and so forth.

He wanted to alleviate that, he wanted to advocate a system that would be productive on a societal level in terms of its advancement of a moral good. That's what was motivating him, I thought.

And I often wonder, when we invoke the name "Adam Smith" to describe economic systems that are based on his orientation, how many people ignore the driving moral undercurrent of his work.

MF: Right. But that said, I'm not sure how many people actually do. Yes, there are heartless plutocrats in the world who really are only concerned with their own enrichment. But when it comes to debates over competing economic systems, we have to give enough credit to both sides to see that, both really do, ultimately, at their best, want to see the kind of profound harm that comes from grinding poverty lessened.

The economically libertarian people I know, like to point out that there is no moral development in the history of humanity of such profound positive magnitude as the degree to which market liberalization in East Asia has brought hundreds of millions of people out of a state of grinding poverty into a state of greater prosperity.

Now, of course, when I as a moral and political theorist, see that a non-democratic oligarchy that has oppressed people in all sorts of ways is the same government that has brought more people out of poverty in China than have ever been brought out of poverty ever before in human history, I have certain moralistic tendencies to say—

HB: OK. But, that's another argument.

MF: Yes.

HB: Right—moving on: you've mentioned Donald Trump on several occasions already throughout this conversation—inevitably twinned with the word "toddler", I've noticed.

MF: Yes. I'm obsessed with current events back in the States right now, I'm losing sleep over them.

HB: This bothers me for two reasons. The first problem is that it irrevocably dates the footage.

MF: Well, if you've had a talk with Quentin Skinner, you know that all ideas are irrevocably dated at the moment of their inception. We are having this conversation on October 14th, 2016, and that will always be true. It may be important to people who watch the video or read the book at some point in the future.

HB: OK, I'm not going to deny that. I guess that brings me to my second point, which is that, generally speaking, I try very hard to avoid talking about Donald Trump, but since you keep bringing him up, and since we are still in advance of next month's presidential election, and since you are a political theorist with a focus on "the real world" who is determined to say relevant things about contemporary politics, it's probably appropriate.

MF: Where are you from, by the way?

HB: I'm Canadian.

MF: People often accuse me of being Canadian as a compliment. I've noticed that whenever British people hear a voice like ours, their first question is, *Are you Canadian?* Because they know that an American will be complimented—or at least an American who lives in Britain.

HB: Don't get me started with Canadians. I'm not a big fan of them, as it happens.

MF: I don't think I've ever met a self-hating Canadian before.

HB: I'm not self-hating. I'm just not generally fond of Canadians. There's a difference.

MF: Okay.

HB: Getting back to Donald Trump, some people might say, "*Well, look, you're advocating that our understanding of the Enlightenment should be broader. Here we have a populist. He's not the only populist in the world right now, but he's certainly the most notorious populist at present who is arguably preying on people's emotions and saying things that are in many ways blatantly irrational. Shouldn't we be thinking about orientations that are more rational rather than less* *rational? Don't we want to consign any emotional aspect of anything to a dustbin somewhere, because look, what happens when people start getting out and preying on people's emotions."*

MF: Right. And that really is the political punchline—the real-world upshot of this book is, *No, that's a terrible mistake*. The only way to combat emotional immaturity and selfishness is through emotional maturity, sympathy, compassion, and empathy.

I take great solace in the fact that Barack Obama, when he was asked by, I think it was, the New York Times Book Review, to name his 10 favourite books, he mentioned—maybe it was for political reasons, a sort of triangulation to say something positive about Adam Smith—*The Theory of Moral Sentiments*.

HB: Of course, Barack Obama has actually read books.

MF: Yes. Here's something else that will date this discussion very precisely.

HB: Well, you just mentioned the date. You can't be a whole lot more precise than that.

MF: That's right. And yesterday, Michelle Obama gave the best response to Donald Trump that we've heard in this election so far. It was an incredibly emotional speech, urging people to identify the moments in their lives that bring them into a place where they can see the affront to human decency that Trump represents.

Women may not have to project themselves imaginatively very far to identify with Trump's victims. Men may have to do a little bit more difficult imaginative work. This rhetoric that we've been hearing that's very troublesome in a lot of ways, is all these people saying, "*As the father of a daughter...*" and "*As the child of a mother...*" and "*As the husband of a wife, what Trump says, is unacceptable to me.*"

And interpreted uncharitably, that can mean: *Only white men like me matter, but I happen to have some women in my life I care about. Therefore, I don't like this.*

I think that maybe people who say things like that haven't expanded their circles of empathetic understanding quite far enough, but it's a beginning. You begin with the circle of people closest to you and you work your way out. And maybe at some point you'll be able to empathetically concern yourself with victims of Trump's rhetoric and behaviour who bear very little resemblance to you at all.

If we're to overcome those emotional tendencies that we have, especially during times of fear or uncertainty, to withdraw into our own narrow perspectives as much as possible, the only resources we have that effectively pull people back out of that aren't pure rational argument.

They are grounded in rhetorical appeals to our power, to emotionally connect with people different from ourselves. The best political rhetoric is often very, very emotional, but it's a call to the compassionate sharing of emotion, rather than a call to narrow self-centred fear, let alone hatred. I think it's very, very important—I'm not just trying to promote book sales here.

It's very important that when we think about how we educate people who want to enter into politics as a vocation, that they understand that what they're entering into isn't about the management of self-interested, rational agents and seeing how you can balance interests against one another.

That may be a part of it, but at its most important and its most noble, the political vocation is about inspiration. Too often rhetoric gets identified with emotional manipulation, but there's a kind of emotional evocation that isn't manipulative, but presents people with the realities of others' lived experiences and calls on people to identify with and concern themselves with those emotional experiences.

And the highest pieces of political rhetoric are the ones that expand people's circles for the pursuit of something good, and rally them to oppose themselves to something that would narrow those circles.

So political philosophy can get very abstract and very disconnected from political practice. But I think there are very important takeaway points for political practice from an appreciation of the sentimentalist tradition.

HB: And we're in one of those times right now.

MF: No question. In so far as I'm optimistic right now, it's because I think we're at this very moment seeing an expansion of empathetic concern going on in American political discourse.

I think there are lots of criticisms you can make of what the British left and the Labour Party are doing right now and why they're so profoundly ineffective. But the inability to use the full repertoire of tools available to get people to broaden their concern is something that worries me about British politics right now.

Now, certainly Clinton herself is not very good at this. But the fact that someone in the Democratic Party has gotten the memo on the importance of the moral sentiments to political life makes me cautiously optimistic for what's going on in the States right now.

HB: Yeah. That seems like a great point to end on. Thank you very much, Michael. It's been a very enjoyable conversation.

MF: Very much so, very much so. I envy your job, that this is what you do. How long were we talking for?

HB: Two and a half hours.

MF: Wow.

Questions for Discussion:

1. How do you think Michael would evaluate the impact of the Trump era on American popular sentiment in terms of "circles of empathetic understanding"?

2. Do you think that Howard's strong judgement of economists is fair? How might an economist respond to his criticism?

3. Do you agree with Michael's assessment that statements like, "As a father of a daughter, what Trump says is unacceptable to me" indicate a certain lack of empathetic concern, albeit "a good start"?

Continuing the Conversation

Readers are encouraged to read Michael's book, *The Enlightenment of Sympathy* which goes into considerable additional detail about many of the issues discussed during this conversation.

Democratic Lessons

What the Greeks Can Teach Us

A conversation with Josiah Ober

Introduction

Back to the Future

How can we make our democracy work better?

Can we give citizens a stronger voice in public affairs? Can we make people more invested in the decisions that are taken? Can we find a way to make better decisions to start with?

Age-old questions, to be sure. And for many, any serious investigation of democracy starts far back in time, in the world of Classical Athens, where the whole idea of democracy was first invented and put into practice.

Of course, we realize now, those early democratic pioneers made many blatant errors in the way they went about doing things. Women, for example, were excluded from participating in all decision-making. So too were slaves, who made up a shockingly large portion of their society.

There was clearly lots wrong with the way things were done some 2500 years ago. But what, it's worth asking, was done particularly right? Can those ancient Greeks help us with our political struggles today?

Josh Ober thinks so.

The Mitsotakis Professor in the School of Humanities and Science at Stanford University, he is an active presence in both the Political Science and Classics Departments and has, by his own admission, "always had some taste for 'ancient meets modern', thinking about how antiquity may shed some light on something that we care about today."

But the key spark to his groundbreaking 1989 book, *Mass and Elite in Democratic Athens: Rhetoric, Ideology and the Power of the People*, happened almost by accident.

> *"I was reading for my dissertation on military changes after the Peloponnesian War, and I came across a couple of passages of the orator Demosthenes that I just didn't understand. He seemed to be contradicting himself in a single speech: making comments that were blatantly elitist—talking about his opponent being this lower-class guy who didn't really deserve the attention of the Athenian citizens—but at the same time saying that his opponent was this guy who pandered to the elite and didn't care about the ordinary people.*

> *"I thought to myself, **How do you get away with that?** How do you get away with being both, 'I'm more elite than my opponent,' and also, 'I'm more of a regular guy than my opponent'? There's got to be something going on here."*

What was going on, he later came to appreciate, was that a close reading of public rhetoric could provide deep insights on aspects of the prevailing political and societal structure that had hitherto gone largely unrecognized.

> *"The basic argument was that political communication in Athens was not a one-way street from elite speaker to mass audience, which was the way it had often been portrayed.*

> *"The speakers had to be intensely attuned to their audience. They had to claim that, 'I'm worthy of listening to **because**,' and then quickly come up with a sufficiently good reason. And they'd also have to say, "My interests are aligned with the interests of our country, of our community, of you the ordinary people, **because**..." and then they'd have to fill that in very quickly as well, before adding, 'And here's my proposal.'*

> *"If you don't do that right in Athens— if you either seem to be somebody who might be perfectly well-intentioned but doesn't know anything more than the ordinary guy, people will think, Why are we listening to you? We need to listen to somebody who knows something.*

"But if the speaker says, 'Oh yeah, I'm an expert. Shut up, you lowly rabble and listen to your superiors,' the masses will naturally have a feeling that this guy's interests aren't terribly well aligned with theirs.

In either case they're going to shout that guy down. The Athenian speakers in the law courts, as well as in these legislative assemblies, had to align what they say with the interests of the people and prove their alignment through what they said, through discourse. They also had to demonstrate their elite credentials: 'Here's why I really know something that's worth all of us taking into account.'

Well, all very interesting, you might think. But how is this relevant to contemporary society? A good question—and one that, intriguingly, Josh has given considerable thought to over the years.

"The question then is, how do you get something like that in the modern world? How do you create, instead of the talking heads speaking down to all of us in one-way communication, a way in which the people, the citizenry, can talk back to those in leadership positions and test them—not just once every four years in an election, but every time they open their mouths?"

Social media and other technological tools, he suggests, may play a pivotal role here. So, too, might more innovative social-science techniques to coherently promote public understanding such as deliberative polling, an invention of his Stanford colleague James Fishkin.

But Josh's key insight is that the ancient Athenians didn't just happen to stumble upon the idea of democracy—they somehow managed to make it work in practice for the better part of 200 years, all the while facing many of the same divisive societal pressures that we are currently grappling with.

After all, the Athenians, too, had enormously wealthy individuals who were constantly striving to "buy" their way into a disproportional share of political power, just as our high-profile political activists and well-funded lobby groups.

The Athenians, too, had a cadre of self-proclaimed elites who were convinced that they ought to be perpetually guiding the mindless rabble.

And yet, despite these constant pressures, Athenian democracy survived and prospered. Which swiftly prompts us to ask, **What, exactly, were they doing right? And how can we learn from them?**

> *"For me, from the very beginning the key question was how to explain why democracy was such a success. The old question scholars used to ask was, Why doesn't it last forever? My question was, **Why does it last for more than twenty minutes?***

> *"There were many reasons to think how it might not have lasted given the structure of ancient democracies, especially if you consider the fact that this was a world in which there were people who were quite privileged—it was not a world that had eliminated inequality, or even pretended to have eliminated inequality, in economic terms, access to education or other areas.*

> *"How do you actually create a world in which elites and masses coexist over time under the majoritarian system of rule? Under what circumstances could the majority of ordinary Athenians accept leadership from elites, without simply turning over the system to them, without falling into what political scientists call now 'elite capture'?*

> *"I think this is why it's worth looking at a society that was democratic for a couple of hundred years, a society that **did** restrain elite capture. This was a society that lived with wealth inequality, but kept it from simply being translated into power inequality in a one-to one way.*

> *"I also think it's worth asking if there are ways, at a much greater scale than anything present in a Greek city state, we could do something similar. Are there institutional mechanisms? Discursive mechanisms? Are there ways to change the nature of culture or education that would at least push back against that, as I see it, double evil of the elites running everything in their own interest, and wealth inequality being directly translated into political inequality?"*

George Santayana famously said, "*Those who don't remember the past are condemned to repeat it.*" The lesson here is somewhat different —more like, "*Those who don't remember the past are missing a great opportunity to improve the present.*"

Not as catchy, perhaps, but likely just as important. Either way, it's clearly worth paying attention to what has happened before. And to ask why.

The Conversation

I. Cutting One's Wisdom Teeth

How a girlfriend's dental work leads to Thucydides

HB: I read an interview with you a while ago where you made a reference to how going to college was a somewhat serendipitous occurrence for you. What was all that about?

JO: If you go back far enough, you get back to the ancient history of the 1960s, which is where things start for me. I was not a particularly motivated student when I was in high school. There were a lot of other things going on that I found much more interesting.

I was living with my girlfriend in the dicier part of Minneapolis at the time, and she developed a problem with her wisdom teeth. Her parents used this to leverage her into college.

HB: How did they do that?

JO: They said they'd pay for the operation she needed if she signed up for courses at the University of Minnesota. So she did.

HB: Otherwise she would have had to deal with the dental problems herself?

JO: That's right. *"Either you can deal with it yourself, or you can do what we want and you will start taking classes at the university."* It wasn't really so bad; they had leverage and they used it. After all, they wanted the best for her. They didn't want her to be living her life with her degenerate boyfriend in the shabby part of Minneapolis.

HB: But little did they know...

JO: That's right. So I decided I would take some classes too. I'd been urged by various friends to give it a try. I figured I may as well do it.

In my first term, I discovered a course in Greek history taught by a fellow called Thomas Kelly who turned out to be my undergraduate advisor. I just thought it was the greatest thing. It was wonderful. It was an introductory class in Greek history, and at the very beginning he went up to the blackboard—this was in the days when there were still blackboards—and he started writing out slowly T-h-u-c-... After he wrote out *Thucydides* in full, he turned to us and said, "*You see this? If you misspell that, you fail the course.*"

It was a big class, and people started laughing. But he just repeated, "*If you misspell this, you fail the course.*" And I thought to myself, *Ah, he's serious!*

This was back in the days when everybody was talking about being "relevant", and many people thought, Well, maybe the kids really **do** know what's going on. Not this guy. He didn't dislike the youth. He just thought Thucydides was more worth paying attention to than most of the burble that was being said by us.

HB: Or most people, for that matter.

JO: Exactly. Or most people ever since.

He just wanted us to take it seriously, and knew how to get our attention. After the end of this first term, I thought, *This stuff is really great. I think I'll do this for a living—why not?* So I went to talk with him during his office hours, and said, "*I really like this; and I'd like to know if you think this would be a good career for me.*"

He looked at me and said, "*You can't.*"

"*Well, why not?*" I asked.

And he replied, "*Well, look at you. You're not going to do what's necessary. You'd have to work much harder than I think you're willing to, so don't waste my time.*"

That was, to his mind, the end of it. But I got a bit stubborn and said, "*Just in case I **were** willing to do the work, what would I have to do?*"

"*Well, you'd have to sign up next term for Greek.*"

He naturally figured that was the end of it for me. But I signed up the next term for Greek and Latin courses. Meanwhile, I continued to take history courses from him. One thing led to another, and at a certain point he said, "*You should maybe think about this thing called graduate school.*"

And I said, "*What's that?*" We were so innocent in those days. Now, all my students are pre-professional by the time they're in grade school. Anyway, he recommended that I go study with someone he had studied with, and that's how I got into the field.

HB: What was the reaction from other people? What was the reaction from your girlfriend with the dental work, or was she still your girlfriend at that point?

JO: That relationship didn't last very long. She decided that she didn't much like going to college, and thought I was wasting my time with it. This was a whole world of ultimatums, I guess. After I'd been there a couple of terms, she told me, "*If you sign up for courses in the spring term, then it's over between us.*"

And I said, "*Then it's over.*" And that was that.

I started hanging out with people who were in the Classics department—undergraduates and some graduate students. They were very supportive. After all, they thought that what we were all doing was great fun.

Some of the professors were more or less supportive. There was an odd division at Minnesota at that point between the historians of antiquity and the classicists. There was some friction back and forth there.

"*What are you doing taking this classics course?*" I remember once being asked by one of the professors (not Tom Kelly). "*It's okay to take Greek and Latin, you need to know that, but we don't want you taking any of their other classes. It rots your mind.*"

If you were going to be serious about doing ancient history, you had to learn the languages, but this was about it. The course in question was taught by a very interesting guy, a sort of runaway Marxist, and it was called "Madness and Sexuality in the Ancient World". So this stuffy professor of ancient history basically looked at that and said, "*They rot your mind over there.*" Well, maybe they did.

HB: It depends on how you define "rot your mind", I suppose.

JO: Exactly.

HB: One more thing before we move on with your academic career. By today's standards, it seems strange that one could have a girlfriend who decides to go to university and then suddenly decide at the last minute, "*Maybe I should go too.*" I'm guessing that's quite a bit harder to do these days than it was in the past.

JO: I think so. Obviously now the whole run-up to applying for university is a huge thing. Certainly my students here at Stanford, and those previously at Princeton, had spent much of their childhood and young adulthood trying to do what it takes to get into the right university. That wasn't an issue for me. I was very lucky that, at that point, the public universities, great state universities, were still relatively open door. I had good enough grades as a high school student, so they let me in, they gave me a shot.

The tuition was almost nothing at that point as well, so the costs of entry were low. It allowed people to try. Lots of people—like my girlfriend at the time, who was really a brilliant person—were able to give it a shot. She tried it for a while and decided that it wasn't how she wanted to spend her life, so she went on to do other things.

But it allowed somebody like me to say, at the last minute, "*Well, maybe I'll give it a try*". And it turned out that it took. Sadly, I think that's much harder to do nowadays. I don't know that it's impossible, but the chance of moving into a kind of serious research university like the University of Minnesota, and then being able to just step into a class with a major scholar like Tom Kelly, is probably not available to most people on that kind of short notice. All of this came together for me in July or August before the fall semester.

HB: That late?

JO: Yes. You had to take an exam at a fixed date. I remember that I had a broken-down car at that point, and the exam was some distance away. As I was ready to leave, I turned the key, and the car didn't start. Luckily, this had happened a couple of weeks before and a friend had shown me a trick of how to jigger the carburetor to get it going. So when I did that, the car started and I went off to take the exam. But if that hadn't happened, then I might not have been able to sign up for those classes. There are all these kinds of serendipitous things that happened.

HB: That's a good reason right there to have friends who know something about cars.

JO: Exactly. That should be a lesson to everyone: talk with people who know something about cars. If you spend all your life hanging around pointy-headed intellectuals who don't know how to fix anything in the real world, then the rest of your life may not go so well.

Questions for Discussion:

1. How much of a role do you think serendipity really plays in our life trajectory? Do you think that Josh would have found a way to become a scholar simply due to his innate disposition?

2. Do you think that people are generally too focused on their careers from an early age on these days? Are there broader societal benefits to enabling people to find their true passions?

II. Digging Deeper

Contrasting wars and lurking contradictions

HB: I'd like to move shortly to political issues, discussing and comparing present-day democracy with that of the Ancient Greeks. But a bit more personal history first: my understanding is that your earlier research was more focused on military history—field archaeology and that sort of thing. It was quite a bit removed from what you later went on to do.

JO: Yes, in a way it was. You have to remember that we move now from the 1960s into the 1970s and the era of the Vietnam War. The war was a huge thing for my generation of Americans. Once again, serendipity was at play. I might well have served in Vietnam but I got a good lottery number, so I didn't have to.

But the whole experience of the state at war, and then the defeat of the United States—which those of us who had been opposing the war recognized it to be—was a really big deal. I was interested in the impact of losing a war on a democratic state. That was the impulse behind my dissertation, which was on Athenian military policy after the Peloponnesian War.

HB: So there were immediate parallels for you between Classical Athens and the Peloponnesian War and the United States and the Vietnam War.

JO: Yes. It wasn't like I was trying to write the US onto Athens.

HB: Given the times, you couldn't *not* make the association, presumably.

JO: Absolutely. The experience of war, a long and difficult and unsuccessful war, and what happens then to the citizens and residents of a country in the aftermath of that kind of defeat, was very much on my mind. It was on the mind of some of my contemporaries as well.

I was just reminiscing the other day with a friend who teaches at Cornell who also does Greek history. He wrote a dissertation that had some of the same kinds of features, although he was interested more directly in Athenian politics. But he had the same impulse: we needed to try to understand what happens to a democratic state in the aftermath of military failure.

This had a naturally political flavour: I got deeply into the question of how Athenians organized their military system—especially how they sought to protect their countryside in the period after the Peloponnesian War—basically because they'd lost an empire. In the previous period, the 5th century, they had an empire and could import everything they wanted. They lose the war, they lose the empire, and therefore they were thrown back on their own resources and now needed to defend the resources in their countryside in addition to just the walled city.

It also got archaeological, because the way you prove that this is what happened is by studying the remains of field fortifications in the countryside around Athens.

HB: Are there are quite a lot of those still?

JO: Yes: there are quite a lot of those. Well, there were at the time, anyway. In the late 1970s there were places you could find that had been noted by earlier archaeologists, or sometimes by attentive travellers in the 19th century. They were clear enough about where they were that if you worked carefully with maps and talked with people and spent a lot of time tramping around in the hills, you could find them and then map out these sites and study them.

In the late 1970s there were still things to be found. You could make a guess that there could be the remains of something on such and such a hill because it would relate to some other remains that you had found. And sometimes you'd find completely new things.

This isn't an excavation, you understand: it's just looking for surface remains.

It was lots of fun and extremely exciting; I did it for years. I thought it was going to be my career, alternating between archaeology and history: using archaeology to explain certain historical developments.

But then, moving forward into the early 1980s, for political reasons the Greek government changed its policies and decided not to allow field permits for foreigners for a while. So the field project that I had raised some money for, and gathered a team for, ground to a halt. And I decided that it was time to do something else.

So that was another career change because of external factors. I realized that if I wanted to go on and get tenure and so on I couldn't depend on the vagaries of the Greek Archaeological Service.

HB: It's clear that there was a strong pragmatic aspect associated with your change of research focus.

But I'm also guessing that some questions were rattling around in your head for some time in terms of how the ancient Athenian democracy lasted as long as it did, the balance of power between the elite and the everyday guy on the street, and so forth.

JO: Yes, I'd been thinking about this pretty seriously for a long time.

This goes back into deep personal history again. I went to a pretty difficult high school. It's a long story, but it was ostensibly a voluntary transfer into quite a troubled high school. My upbringing had been a relatively comfortable middle-class American one, and transferring into this school in which there were a lot of kids who weren't comfortable middle-class Americans was a real eye-opening experience for me.

I became very interested in the whole idea of how those who are not among the elite, or not even among the middling, relate to elites. At that point I knew people who had received very elite educations, going to private schools and so on. That's another girlfriend story, but we'll skip that.

HB: No dental work involved?

JO: No dental work involved in that one, no.

HB: But in short, you became quite sensitive to this notion of the haves and have-nots from personal experience.

JO: That's right. This was really quite pointed for me.

And years later, as I was reading for my dissertation on military changes after the Peloponnesian War, I came across a couple of passages of the orator Demosthenes that I just didn't understand. He seemed to be contradicting himself in a single speech: making comments that were blatantly elitist—talking about his opponent being this lower-class guy who didn't really deserve the attention of the Athenian citizens—but at the same time saying that his opponent was this guy who pandered to the elites and didn't care about the ordinary people.

I thought to myself, *How do you get away with **that**? How do you get away with being both, "**I'm more elite than my opponent**," and also, "**I'm more of a regular guy than my opponent**"? There's got to be something going on here.*

I was sensitive to this issue because, as I said, I had long been interested in how some people make claims to elite privilege that others simply can't.

That began a side project of collecting notes on what I called to myself at that point *Elitism and Anti-elitism in Athenian Thought*. And that's what I turned to within a month of getting turned down for the permit to do the archaeological work. I embarked on this elitism and anti-elitism project.

HB: I see. And I'm guessing that one of the advantages of that whole approach is that there were lots of texts available. If you want to look at the art of rhetoric, what people were doing and how they were engaging with the masses and so forth, you could really do a comprehensive, systematic study of that over a long period of time.

JO: That's absolutely right. As a graduate student, I'd become very interested in political rhetoric—the way in which speakers to large, democratic audiences make claims.

The first article I ever published was on views of sea power in the 4th century (BCE) Attic orators. I'd read the orators carefully and I had the idea that there was more to them than just representing a mine of historical facts, or a way to think about Greek prose, which was the way that it had been primarily studied in the past.

I had this intuition that by thinking about what the orators are saying and not saying, examining contradictions—well, what seemed to be contradictions to me, anyway—there would be a way to understand more deeply how the Athenians thought about important things—initially military history and sea power, but then more broadly the role of elites and non-elites within a democratic society.

HB: Were you thinking then about connecting this with the longevity of the Athenian democratic system?

I'm not a classicist, of course, but it seems to me that one doesn't get confronted with those sorts of questions early on, at the introductory stages of Greek history. Rather there's a sense of, "*Oh, those wonderful Greeks*, (and it's usually "those Greeks", rather than "those Athenians" as opposed to "those Spartans" or "those Corinthians" or whatever), *they had this brilliant idea of democracy, which lives on today.*"

Aside from the fact that the Greeks were hardly universally democratic at that time, there are also the questions, *How did this actually work? Why did democracy last for as long as it did?*

When you started looking at these texts and examining the rhetoric, were you already thinking about somehow probing that, looking for insights into these bigger questions of stability of the Athenian democratic system?

JO: Yes, I was.

I mean, my generation of Greek historians changed the nature of the question about the period after the Peloponnesian War. Instead of seeing that as the period of decline and failure, which is the way that it had been often portrayed, we tended to think that the remarkable thing is how vibrant a society we have. Look how well Athens recovers from the war, look what happens in the Greek world in this post-war world.

For me, from the very beginning the key question was how to explain why democracy was such a success, rather than why it was such a failure. The old question was, *Why doesn't it last forever?* My question was, *Why does it last for more than twenty minutes?*

There were many reasons to think how it might not have, given the structure of ancient democracies, especially if you consider the fact that this was a world in which there were people who were quite privileged—it was not a world that had eliminated inequality, or even pretended to have eliminated inequality, in economic terms, access to education or other areas.

How do you actually create a world in which elites and masses coexist over time under the majoritarian system of rule? Under what circumstances could the majority of ordinary Athenians accept leadership from elites, without simply turning over the system to them, without falling into what political scientists call now "elite capture"?

Questions for Discussion:

1. Does the engagement in archaeology, such as Josh describes, give historians a somewhat different perspective on the past? To what extent do you think his past archaeological activities influence his future research?

2. How do you think future historians would evaluate our society based on a close examination of current rhetorical practices?

3. To what extent do you think America's Founding Fathers were worried about "elite capture"? How do you think they would judge contemporary American society from that perspective?

III. Battling Iron Laws

Athenian democracy as a counterexample

HB: One of the things that I'm keen on exploring is the relevance of your work on classical Athenian democracy to what's going on today. Earlier we spoke of the parallels, or at least potential parallels, between the Vietnam War and Peloponnesian War.

When you started this work, were you already motivated to look for general truths about the democratic process, insofar as how they may or may not relate to any democracy, including the one we're in now?

Let me be more explicit. My understanding of Thucydides is that he was one of these historians who believed very strongly in the relevance of history to help future generations. "*Here are the signs of the plague,*" he seems to be telling us, "*Remember these details so that if, say, 300 years from now, people reading this should come across something similar, you'll be able to identify it for what it is.*"

Were you influenced by Thucydides, or your own particular views, to the extent that you started thinking that way as well? Were you thinking, "*Hey, here's a sort of test case for democracy. Well, I live in a democracy that is hardly perfect right now. Maybe I can learn something...*" Were you thinking of extrapolating key moments from the past to the present right from the very beginning?

JO: Yes, I really was. I've always had some taste for "ancient meets modern", thinking about how antiquity may shed some light about something we care about today.

Early in my career, I was fortunate to get a job at Montana State University out of graduate school. I was allowed to take a leave to a research centre, where I was lucky enough to talk with some really smart social scientists who helped me see the ways in which the kind of questions I was asking were, in fact, related to the kind of questions social scientists were currently asking.

Pretty early on, I started to think of this project about masses and elites, or elitism and anti-elitism, as a way to test the so-called "iron law of oligarchy", a theory that had been really important in social science since the early 20th century when it was first devised by Robert Michels.

The iron law of oligarchy says that behind every form of government or political organization there will be an oligarchy, or that an oligarchy will emerge whether you start out with a monarchy or a democracy—you will quickly devolve to an oligarchy: it's a necessary consequence of the nature of human organizations.

Michels had been a socialist studying political parties in Germany and elsewhere, and his studies showed him that the socialist parties of Europe ultimately were taken over by elites. He was depressed by this, but ended up reconciling himself with it, deciding that the fascists in Italy had it right after all.

HB: That's a different story, I guess.

JO: Yes, and a sad one. Initially, I think he was hoping to find different results, but he became convinced by his own social science that this was simply the way the world went.

I was very interested to test that. It looked to me—and still looks to me—as if Classical Athens had not fallen to this iron law. So then the question is, *why*? Under what circumstances, under what conditions, would you be able to maintain a really robust democracy in which ordinary citizens really *do* keep purchase on the sayings and doings of elites?

And that seemed to me to be hugely important, because if you get one example where an "iron law" doesn't seem to hold, you prove it is not an **iron** law.

HB: It's a counterexample.

JO: That's right: one counterexample eliminates it from being an "iron law". You can still say that it's a *general tendency*, but you can no longer say that it's something that's *inevitable* and therefore it's foolish to imagine otherwise.

HB: Especially if your counterexample is as salient, and as notable in democratic history, as classical Athenian democracy. I mean, that's a pretty big counterexample.

JO: Yes, that's always been the great advantage I've had in talking with other social scientists and humanists: everybody's heard of this one. You don't have to say, "*Well, I've got a really obscure example that we don't know much about, but from the few things we think we know...*"

We know *a lot* about it. It has a certain claim to being the first large-scale, well-documented democracy. So if we can disprove **this** "iron law" with Classical Athens, then we've done some real work. And that's much of what I've been focused on ever since.

Questions for Discussion:

1. Can you think of any other historical counterexamples to the "iron law of oligarchy"?

*2. To what extent is it reasonable to assume that any sorts of "iron laws" of human behaviour actually exist? In what way does this very notion assume an equivalence in approach between the social and natural sciences? (Those interested in exploring different perspectives on this concept are referred to Chapters 3–4 of the Ideas Roadshow conversation **How Social Science Creates the World** with UC Berkeley political theorist Mark Bevir.)*

IV. Feet to the Fire?

Using new and old media to keep politicians on point

HB: I'd like to turn now to exploring some of the details of your analysis and investigate to what extent it is relevant to today's world.

As I understand it, one aspect from *Mass and Elite in Democratic Athens* is this idea of discourse, this interchange. Earlier you highlighted Demosthenes and his tools of rhetoric, how he—or presumably any orator or politician—is interacting with the body politic, with the mass of individuals, and vice-versa. This interaction, this discourse, is an essential aspect of a thriving and stable democratic system.

When I look at that from the perspective of today, it seems to me that we are obviously in a different circumstance because we need intermediaries. We aren't involved in regularly making arguments to large gatherings of people, or listening to others making them. Those intermediaries, it seems to me, are represented today by what we call the media.

Is that right? Does that analogy hold? And if so, is the media fulfilling its role in this regard?

JO: The basic argument of the book on mass and elites was that political communication in Athens was not a one-way street from elite speaker to mass audience, which was the way it had often been portrayed.

The way the Athenians made their rules was by gathering in a large assembly of several thousand citizens. A lottery-chosen council would have set an agenda for the meeting. Then the guy who was chosen as president of the assembly for a day would say, through a herald, "*Here's the agenda: war or peace with Sparta, raise taxes or lower taxes*" or whatever it was. And then he'd ask, "*Who, of the Athenians, has advice to give?*"

At this point, some of the people who were, in a sense, full-time politicians—although in the period I was primarily dealing with, the 4th century BCE, these were not people holding offices—would be clustered around the front near the speaker's platform, saying, "*I do! I do!*"

One of them would get recognized and go up to the speaker's platform. And he would get to speak for exactly as long as the Athenians were willing to listen to him, which might be 15 seconds, or it might be 10 or 15 minutes. But it wouldn't be longer than that. Then somebody else would get recognized, and so on.

The guy would speak for as long as he was saying things that the audience thought were worth hearing. And as soon as he did not say that, he would simply be shouted down. As one individual without amplification, you're forced to speak to a very large audience in this large, theatrical area. You can be heard, but not if several thousand people are saying, "*Sit down you idiot, let somebody who really knows something say something.*"

The whole point is that the speakers had to be intensely attuned to their audience. They had to claim that, "*I'm worthy of listening to **because**,*" and then quickly come up with a sufficiently good reason.

And they'd also have to say, "*My interests are aligned with the interests of our country, of our community, of you the ordinary people, **because**...*" and then they'd have to fill that in very quickly as well, before adding, "*And here's my proposal.*"

If you don't do that right in Athens—if you either seem to be somebody who might be perfectly well-intentioned but doesn't know anything more than the ordinary guy, people will think, *Why are we listening to you? We need to listen to somebody who knows something.*

But if the speaker says, "*Oh yeah, I'm an expert. Shut up, you lowly rabble and listen to your superiors,*" the masses will naturally have a feeling this guy's interests aren't terribly well aligned with theirs.

In either case they're going to shout him down.

That was the basic idea in this mass and elite book. The Athenian speakers in the law courts, as well as in these legislative assemblies, had to align what they say with the interests of the people and prove their alignment through what they said, through discourse. They also had to demonstrate their elite credentials—*"Here's why I really know something that's worth all of us taking into account."*

The question then is, *How do you get something like that in the modern world?* How do you create, instead of the talking heads speaking down to all of us in one-way communication, a way in which the people, the citizenry, can talk back to those in leadership positions and test them—not just once every four years in an election, but every time they open their mouths—because the people were voting on pretty much everything in Athens.

So to return to your question, we can ask, *What role does the media have in all of that?* They can certainly help to assess the credentials of the people in leadership positions. They can answer why I should listen to one particular politician rather than another. If the media have done their job, I will believe that this person has certain credentials, certain expertise, and certain abilities. The same thing is true if I'm wondering if this individual's interests are aligned with my own. Once again, if the media do their job, they can show me how that's either true or false.

But then, how do I, as an individual, actually get *purchase*? Suppose I say, *"All right, I'll let you start speaking,"* because the media have shown me that there's reason to let you start speaking. How do I now jump in with my fellow citizens to say, *"Now you're getting off the point. Now you seem to be deviating, and so we'd like to hear someone else's opinion on this, thank you very much."* That's not as obvious.

Here I'm at Stanford, where there are people who know a whole lot more than I do about how social media is working and might work. I think that there are potentially ways to imagine social media taking a role in talking back to politicians. In fact, I think that's actually beginning to happen already, although the eventual outcomes are not yet clear.

I think that politicians these days are trying to figure out how to use and respond to social media. The official media are also trying to figure out how to use and respond to social media. I think we're in a time when nobody really knows very clearly the answer to those questions. I don't either, but I think it's incumbent upon all of us to be thinking hard about it.

Questions for Discussion:

1. *To what extent are scale factors important in politics? Might it be impossible to recreate an ancient Athenian political environment simply because modern democracies are dealing with vastly different numbers of people?*

2. *How do corporate and political interests influence the media's role in assessing credentials that Josh mentions in this chapter? To what extent can or should this be regulated?*

V. Why Athens?

Addressing elite capture and economic and political inequality

HB: Let me be devil's advocate for a moment. I see that, in principle, we might be able to use technology, social media or otherwise, to have this feedback loop from the people back to the politicians.

But I might say, *"Well, that's all well and good, but the Greeks did something different from what we're doing now. Why should we necessarily want to be doing that? What makes this the optimal way to move forward in a democracy?"*

There seems to be an assumption there that this is the way a democracy *should* be, that the ancient Greeks represent some abstract, universal norm that we've deviated from and must correct somehow using our new technology. So convince me that should necessarily be the case.

JO: There are really two ways to think about it. One is the problem of elite capture. The other is economic inequality that turns into political inequality. I think that both of these are really live issues today. I think most Americans would be quite unhappy with the idea that, *"The way it's going, and will continue to go, is that the people who are running Washington, the people who are running your world, don't really have to listen to you anymore. They're the real ones who are in power."*

HB: Punctuated by this symbolic 'voting event' every four years...

JO: Yes, voting in periodic elections is a weak way for citizens to call political leaders to account.

So what if we concluded, "*In short, the elites figured out how to end-run any real input from the rest of us, so I'm afraid we're all just going to have to live with it.*"

I think if it was put in those terms to the American citizens, they would tend to say, "*I don't want to live with it.*" Maybe they'd say, "*That's the way it's going, we just have to.*" But I think they would feel that there's something awful if you describe what elite capture is, and tell them that it's what we've got, or what we're getting, and there's no way around it. I think there would be a sense of, "*Gee, that's not the way it's supposed to go.*"

Then suppose we added the claim that, "*Although it may have always been the case that some people in our country have more wealth and more influence, it's now going to be completely uncapped. The most powerful people are going to be the wealthiest people, and you will be exactly as important as your paycheck. So if somebody has a thousand times your wealth, they're effectively a thousand times better person than you. Live with it.*"

I think that most members of a democratic society would have a visceral reaction to this of, "*No, that's wrong. Okay fine, this person is a thousand times wealthier than I am—maybe she earned it, maybe she didn't. But she isn't a thousand times **better person** than I am. She shouldn't have a thousand times **more influence** in the society than I do.*"

Once again, I think that there would be a sense that it would be really wrong if that's the way things ended up.

That's the reason to talk about how the citizenry of a democratic society might restrain the elite from this kind of robust form of capture and restrain political inequality from following economic inequality, which is what many fear is presently happening today and will continue to happen into the future.

And that's the reason why I think it's worth looking at a society that was democratic for a couple of hundred years, a society that **did** restrain elite capture. This was a society that did live with wealth inequality, but kept wealth inequality from simply being translated into power inequality in a one-to-one way.

I also think it's worth asking if there are ways, at a much greater scale than anything present in a Greek city state, we could do something similar. Are there institutional mechanisms? Discursive mechanisms? Are there ways to change the nature of culture or education that would at least push back against the, as I see it, double evil of the elites running everything in their own interest, and wealth inequality being directly translated into political inequality?

HB: Do you think that there is that frustration building here in the United States, the frustration that, *"We're well and truly on the road to elite capture and that our democracy is being perverted"*?

Here's my personal problem with this. I wholeheartedly agree with what you're saying. But as an external observer, I don't see the anger and the frustration that one might expect to see, given how this society has changed over the last 25 years in terms of income inequality, wealth disparity, and clear signs of oligarchic developments at all sorts of different political levels. I know there have been movements here and there, like *Occupy Wall Street*, but by and large I don't get a sense of real social turmoil.

Moreover, if there really **was** the sort of anger and frustration around that we're talking about, I'm guessing that people would first take a more active look around them at other contemporary states, rather than necessarily examining ones from the distant past. They would ask, *"Well, how's Sweden handling things? Is Germany doing better on these vital matters than we are?"*

But I don't get the sense that people are concerned very much about this. I don't get a sense that there is that sort of anger and concern on the street.

But maybe I'm wrong. Do you? And do you feel that there's enough attention being paid to other contemporary social structures and governments?

JO: I don't know how to measure this, but this represents a nice social-science empirical question about measuring the level of anxiety or despair or anger or frustration. I said that if it were put in these terms to the American people, they would say, *"No, that's horrible, I don't want that."* We should be able to test that empirically.

But it's another question to ask whether it is **now** being put in those stark terms to the American people—I tend to think probably not. It's not in the interest of anybody who wants to achieve elected office to say those sorts of things.

HB: And I'm not sure it's in the media's interest to do this either.

JO: I think that may well be right. They are undergoing huge changes. It's not at all clear whether any newspaper is going to have a viable business model over the next 20 years, or how many of them will. The same thing applies to other forms of serious media, as opposed to purely entertainment media. They are, in some ways, running scared. They want to figure out the next thing, but they don't want to, as it were, kill themselves before they've figured it out.

It's not entirely clear that message is being made in ways that people are taking it up. On the other hand, *Capital in the Twenty-First Century*, Thomas Piketty's extremely technical, huge tome of a book on social inequality—

HB: Is being purchased.

JO: Yes. It's being purchased. And it's also being talked about.

This is one of the most startling things in recent publishing history. Nobody predicted this. I'm fairly certain that Harvard University Press didn't say in advance, *"Ha! We're going to run a thousand academic titles over the next hundred years on the back of this one book; what a clever thing to do!"* I don't think anybody supposed that this was going to happen.

The fact that it **is** getting all of this attention does suggest that at least the issue of structural inequality is one that strongly resonates with the public. I don't want to get too far outside of things I can genuinely claim to know something about, but the natural tendency is to think that the objection is going to come from the left—that's a natural sort of conclusion from someone who grew up in the 1960s and 1970s, protesting the Vietnam War.

But I think that in many ways the Tea Party is channelling a lot of this kind of anger. They don't like the current crop of the elites who are running things. Now, I don't think the Tea Party folks have any solution to the problem—

HB: Fair enough. But you're just answering my question. I asked you about signs of widespread societal anger and frustration about these issues, and you're pointing to a couple.

JO: Yes. So I think that, if you want to look for straws in the wind, and you're willing to look outside of the ordinary places, they are out there.

Regarding where you're going to look in the modern world, I just don't think Europe's going to do it. At the moment, you don't want the European economy. Europe as a federal project is going to take a lot of work. They don't seem to have a very obvious way forward between the people who are advocating more austerity and the ones who are saying austerity is going to kill the possibility of economic growth.

On the other hand, waves of ultra-nationalism are increasingly the big story, at least at the margins of most major European states right now. Not too many people want to say, "*Gosh, that's terrific. All we need are some neo-Nazis to spark up the place.*"

HB: So there's no obvious poster boy?

JO: I don't feel there is. The United States came into existence as the "anti-Europe". We just aren't used to looking over our shoulders and saying, "*Oh well, our elders and betters had it right all along*". I think it's sort of a non-starter to say, "*Gee, Sweden is doing pretty well, so why don't we do things just like Sweden?*"

The United States is a very different place than most European states. We're not an ethno-national state in the same way that European states imagine themselves as being ethno-national states. The United States is famously a mosaic of ethnicities, no one of which can claim to be the soul of the country, as opposed to France for example. That is, whatever your particular colour may be, "Frenchness" is still something that is very tangible.

We don't have the same sort of ethno-national claims here, so we have to do it all based on politics and values. What is it to be American? It is to believe in a certain set of values, not in a basic ethno-national kind of "Americanness"—not that people don't try to do that.

Questions for Discussion:

1. In what ways is the political polarization of contemporary American society related to the issues discussed in this chapter?

2. Do you agree with the claim that the United States came into existence as "the anti-Europe"? What role do you think the notion of "democracy" played in the formation of the American Republic? (Readers particularly interested in these ideas are referred to Chapters 1–3 of the Ideas Road-show conversation **Democracy: Clarifying the Muddle** *with University of Cambridge political theorist John Dunn.)*

3. Is it possible to clearly enunciate the "certain set of values" Josh believes reflective of "being American"? To what extent is this merely a trope that Americans tell themselves, equivalent to a French person's sense of "Frenchness"?

VI. Dissent

Critiquing our system or our values

HB: We talked about modes of communication between the elites and the masses in Classical Athens, thinking about whether or not we might be able to simulate that today using technology so that we don't find ourselves in a situation where the elites just tell us what to do whether we like it or not.

Another fundamental aspect of core democratic principles that you highlight in your work is political dissent. You mention that this is something present over the roughly two hundred years—periodically interrupted—of Athenian democracy: there was a wide spectrum of very important and influential people who were saying all sorts of dissenting things about Athenian democracy, and the society was not only able to absorb that, but perhaps, to a certain extent, actually encourage it.

If you compare and contrast that with the situation today, do you see enough of that around? Are there enough people voicing seriously significant critical views these days—you mentioned Thomas Piketty just a moment ago—that we don't have to worry so much about that? Or is that an issue of concern for you now?

JO: I think that the question of what it is to be a public intellectual, and how important public intellectuals are in the United States, is one that I've thought about a little bit, although it's not my main area.

What I tend to think about the Athenian situation is that the reality of democracy in Athens, and the success of democracy in Athens, is what pushed various elites (like Thucydides or Plato or Aristotle) into a position of having to justify some other form of political organization that would be better than democracy.

My work on dissent essentially said that the whole Western tradition of political thought, to the extent that it's grounded in these texts that were written in Athens by people living in Athens—whether or not they were Athenians by birth—is in part to be explained through the challenge that an effective democracy gave to these aristocratic elites, forcing them to go considerably beyond just saying, "*Well, if the better sort of people were to run things, things would be run rather better around here.*"

As you mentioned, the democracy was interrupted a couple of times in the late 5th century BCE—the "better sort of people" *did* take over, and made a holy mess of the place. That was generally acknowledged, even by Plato, whose relatives were centrally involved with the second of these interruptions.

So it's no longer a self-evident truth that there are a bunch of "better people", the sort of people one goes to dinner parties with, if you're Plato, who, if they were to take the place over, would obviously—because of their intrinsic betterness—do a rather better job of it.

If that's off the table because we tried that and it was a mess, then the question is, *Well, is that all there is to be done? Is democracy as good as it can be?* Maybe not. I think that's what really generates this remarkable explosion of political thought, which in some ways we've been dealing with ever since—some of the great monuments of Western political thought, written just at this time, just at this place.

So I think your question amounts to, *Do we have anything like that now?*

It's not obvious that we do, and partly we don't because we don't have people who are willing to declare themselves to be aristocratic elites like Plato's lot who say, "*Well, there must be some answer to this whole democracy mess*", or "*This democracy thing seems to be going so well, but it surely must be a mess because it can't really be that the rabble would run things better than we would.*"

HB: Well, the modern equivalents might not be so much the die-hard aristocrats, but—at the risk of continually referring to him—people like Thomas Piketty who say, "*We're going off the rails, we're losing our core democratic principles, our egalitarian principles, our moral principles*" or whatever. Dissent can take all sorts of forms.

The idea that our democracy can be subjected to serious negative criticism is presumably, in and of itself, the sign of a healthy democracy—or at least of a healthy structure that can advance.

JO: Right, so there are two ways of thinking about this. One is that the best sort of dissent in a democracy is internal dissent, saying, "*Our democratic values are being violated, and we need to return to those values, perhaps by first clarifying or perfecting them.*"

The other way follows Plato, saying, "*You've got the wrong values. There are better values. The ones that you cherish so, my dear democrat, are actually false values. There are higher and better values.*"

And you can have really great criticism either way.

In the first case, you have criticism that says, "*Let's return to what it really means to be citizens of a democratic state. Let's think about freedom, let's think about equality, and let's think about dignity.*"

I would also welcome the thought that there would be people who would stand outside of the system, and say, "*Let's think about a **different** set of values.*" As it happens, those aren't going to be **my** values—*I'm* going to push against it, but I think this may be one of the big challenges that we're going to see from the rise of China. There's been a lot of discussion recently about whether a whole separate set of values, which are sometimes called Confucian values, or Eastern values—there are all kinds of locutions for this—might be better than our attachment to the "freedom, equality, dignity" triad that lies at the center of democracy. One could imagine, say, obedience, piety and respect for those above you in the hierarchy.

Again, *I* personally don't see a way forward there, but I think it would be a good thing for a democracy to have people who are making these kinds of arguments, so that the democrats are forced to push back against that to explain what they think is wrong with that picture, just as democrats pushed back against the Plato picture or that of the other of the critical elites of Athens.

HB: I have two comments, off the top of my head.

The first is that, in my experience, those who hold the sorts of values you were just describing—who advocate a different set of values based upon obedience or whatever—are by definition not interested in a democratic process of exchange. That is, holding such values typically precludes the idea of having a free and open debate about those very values, it seems to me. Put another way, if you've arranged to hold the keys to the castle, as it were, there's likely not much interest on your end in opening up a debate about whether or not you should.

But I think that there's a very interesting point lurking behind all of this, which is that the idea of the possibility of being able to single out basic human values that we all share, enunciating a set of values that are somehow resonant with the human condition, in principle necessarily diminishes the arguments people might make about different places can hold some different, fundamental values.

Let me give an example to try to clarify what I mean here. When I ask people if there's anything to "Asian values", which I think was the term a couple of decades years ago for what you were alluding to just now—Confucian values, Eastern values and so forth—the standard response I get, at least from those *I* ask, is, "*No no, this is just a trope that people who want to cling to power use, and they don't even necessarily really believe that themselves,*" or "*It's just a mechanism by which they are furthering their own oligarchic cause. They're just saying, 'You have to respect obedience and what we mean by obedience is obedience to us'. They're just trying to justify their hold on power.*"

But then when I push them a little bit by asking, "*Well, does this mean that at some level all societies are the same, that all societies really do believe in a common set of particular values?*" there's usually a fair amount of waffling, because it's fairly clear that at some levels all societies are **not** the same, and stating as much might also jar with their inherent sense of human diversity, or societal relativism or something.

So, now I'm going to put you on the spot a little. Where do you fall, exactly, here? My sense is that you believe in the inherent universal nature of these human values as instantiated by this general democratic framework. Is that a fair description of your beliefs?

JO: Yes, it is fair. This does take us on a slightly different path, though.

HB: I told you the conversation wasn't scripted.

JO: That's right. And I'm very happy to go on that path. I've spent some time thinking about it, and it's really at the core of the next big project I'm hoping to work on.

Questions for Discussion:

1. What do you think "democratic values" are, exactly? To what extent are they commonly shared across one country or a group of countries?

*2. Do "Eastern values" exist? If so, are they substantially different from "freedom, equality and dignity"? (Those interested in different perspectives related to this question are referred to two different Ideas Roadshow conversations: Chapter 4 of **Turning the Mirror: A View From the East** with bestselling author Pankaj Mishra and Chapter 10 of **Byzantium: Beyond the Cliché** with UC Berkeley historian Maria Mavroudi.)*

VII. Enter Aristotle

The perils of being a cat in a box

JO: This is a path that was laid by Aristotle, and really gets us thinking about the whole question of human nature and what kind of beings we are. I should say that I think that you can have all kinds of reasons to prefer democracy to other alternatives, without necessarily going on this Aristotelian path that I'll sketch shortly.

Winston Churchill perhaps gave the most famous reason when he said, *"Democracy is the worst of all possible forms of government, except for all of the other ones that have been tried from time to time."*

So that's a rather diminishing endorsement. Churchill believed in the practical superiority of democracy, but clearly didn't have my sense that there are human-nature reasons to think that it is a good in itself.

But here's the essential Aristotelian argument, which I think is basically right, bracketing the thought that Aristotle made fundamental mistakes in many of his premises. He made mistakes about biology, he made mistakes about human capacity for those who weren't elite, Greek males like he was.

HB: You distinguish between his "useless arguments"—his extra-baggage arguments—and his "valid arguments".

JO: That's right. There are lots of arguments made in Aristotle's great political works—*The Politics* especially—that we can't make any use of. There are some useless arguments, or just baggage that we don't need to carry along.

HB: So perhaps we should say that you're going to enunciate a view that's inspired by Aristotle.

JO: That's right. It's Aristotelian because it comes from reading Aristotle's, but it is not Aristotle's. If Aristotle were here, I think he'd say, *"No no, you don't really understand, you're failing to pay attention to the important bits."* Fine. I don't hold a brief for this being Aristotle's view.

Basically, what Aristotle famously says is that humans are political animals. By this he means that we are a subset of all of the animals in the world, with very specific kinds of features. He divides the animal kingdom into animals that are group-forming, live in groups, and those that live out on their own.

Think about orangutans, for example. They're animals that live individual lives. Obviously they have ways to mate, but they live as individuals. Then you have lots and lots of animals that live in groups: herds of antelope, schools of fish, flocks of birds and troops of primates. And humans.

We're in the group-forming category. It's possible for humans to live alone, as Aristotle points out, but we tend not to do it. We live in societies. We live in groups.

You then take the group-forming animals and further subdivide them. There are those that create public goods, goods in common. Here you have bees and ants, for example: bees create the public good of honey that all the bees of the hive live on, ants gather grains for the colony in similar kinds of ways.

Then, he says, there are humans. He's not doing Darwinian taxonomy here—he's not saying we're descended directly from ants or bees or anything silly like that. He's talking about our behaviour. When we consider what kind of animals we are, we recognize that we're like social insects because we produce public goods that we consume together in a society, such as security or welfare.

Aristotle thought that humans are the most political of all animals, because we produce the most complex forms, and—he also thought—the morally highest forms, of public goods through our unique capacities.

So that's Aristotle's taxonomy: we're super-political animals, and that's why he says humans are political animals. We're the most political of all animals. Not because we're strategic or we form political parties—it's not political in that sense. In fact, he thought that those were unfortunate side-effects of being human.

But rather, we're the most political of animals because we have the capacity to create really rich forms of public goods that benefit each and all of us within a community.

The second idea, then, is that each species of animal—Aristotle doesn't quite think in terms of what we would now call a "species", but that will certainly do for our discussion—has certain capacities that are distinctive to it as a species, as a kind of being, and constitute the individuals of that species as what they are.

Think about a cat. A cat has lots of capacities. It can eat and it can reproduce; it can do things all kinds of animals can do. But it also has some distinctive attributes. For example, a cat pounces on stuff. I have a cat and I tend to think of this as I watch it pounce on things.

Now the idea is that the free exercise of those capacities are good for that kind of being. Imagine, for a moment, that you have a cat and you treat it well in every way—you give it food and affection, keep it warm and so on—but you keep it in a small cage for its entire life.

Anybody who has a cat—if I do this in a public lecture people tend to gasp when I say this—knows that this is a horrible thing to do to a cat. There are other animals that you can easily keep in a smallish cage, and they're fine with it, because they live in burrows or whatever.

HB: But in the case of a cat, you're now eliminating, or at least reducing, its fundamental capacity.

JO: That's right. You are basically not allowing any free exercise of that pouncing capacity that is constitutive of the kind of being it is.

HB: You're not allowing it to flourish.

JO: Right. It fails to flourish, even though it could live a long life. It might be well-fed, plump even, and would show other physical manifestations of being all right. But no one who knows anything about cats would say that what we have here is a flourishing cat that flourished through the course of its life.

And the idea is that each species is like this. It has certain capacities. So, what are the human capacities? Aristotle's very clear about this. We have a kind of a hyper-social capacity, which enables us to make these superior public goods. We have reasoning capacity—that's how we make these goods. We have the capacity to reason abstractly, both towards ends, we would say, for advantage and disadvantage. And we can reason about moral things, about good and evil. Other animals don't have this. He's making a value judgement, but he's not saying that other animals live bad lives for them. He's just saying that these are *our* capacities, which he thinks are higher. He does have a hierarchy.

So we've got hyper-sociability, we've got reasoning capacity and we have communicative ability: we have the ability to use speech, or writing—sophisticated forms of communication. Other animals don't have this.

These are what constitutes us as human. If you take the analogy forward then, in any society or community that *doesn't* give you, as an individual human being, a chance to exercise your hyper-sociability, your reasoning ability, and your communicative ability—

HB: You're going to be a cat in a box.

JO: Right. You're going to be a cat in a box. And if you put hyper-sociability, and reasoning, and communication together, it means that you use your mind and communicate with your fellows towards common ends, towards things that will make it better for us as a society—let's say security or welfare or whatever.

HB: Hence you're a political animal.

JO: Hence you're a political animal; and you're also a *democratic* animal. Because each of us has this capacity. Aristotle is very clear about this. This isn't limited to a few really smart guys and all the rest of us should just sit quietly and take out our tongues. We *each* have this.

Now, as I said before, he makes all of these bad and useless arguments about how women are limited in this, as well as "natural slaves" and so on. But what I would suggest is that we get rid of those bad arguments and just take the "inspired-by Aristotle" view, which I think is right.

Of course, you might think, *Well no, humans* **aren't** *especially sociable*. But that seems to me like an odd sort of thing to say. We are; and we're sociable in ways that other primates aren't. We're sociable in ways that don't require hierarchy all the way down.

If you look at a troop of chimps or gorillas, for example, they require a very strict hierarchy. They can't exist without it. Or they can't exist in a flourishing condition without it. That's just what they are. **We** can. Now, obviously some societies are very hierarchical, all societies have some forms of hierarchy. But when we met, we didn't have to do for example the kind of weird things that chimps have to do—thank god—to determine which of us is the alpha.

We can just *be*. That's distinctive.

But to say that humans aren't hyper-sociable, would be to make a mistake. And to say that humans don't have a reasoning capacity that is different from, or at least different at some level than, other animals, would also be to make a mistake. Clearly other animals can reason to some extent from means to ends, but humans obviously have a reasoning capacity that's different.

And, once again, there's communication. Other species do communicate one way or another, but no other species communicates with the level of complexity that we do.

If you buy the basic argument—and this is what people might not buy—that exercise of constitutive capacities, free exercise, is good for a being, then I think that you've backed yourself into the democratic corner.

I find that to be a pretty hard argument to think myself out of, without saying that humans are just completely different from all other kinds of animals. You'd have to somehow claim that, while for other animals the exercise of their constitutive capacities—like the cat being out of the cage—is good for them, but for us it's not good for us for some peculiar reason. I just don't understand why we wouldn't be like animals in that way, that the free exercise of our constitutive capacities is good for us.

HB: It certainly seems tautological. I mean, once you say "constitutive capacities," it seems to me that you're implying something fundamental that needs to be fulfilled in order to flourish.

JO: Yes. So, you can come up with other capacities. You could say, "*Well, fine, we've got those; but what **really** constitutes us as human is our capacity to be obedient to another human.*" Somebody could use this kind of argument and say, "*Actually, you've got the capacities wrong.*"

But I'm just following along with Aristotle and saying that I think he had them right. He didn't have them right because he was trying from the get-go to make a good argument about democracy—indeed, he was one of the critics of democracy.

HB: Right. It's simply a logical consequence of his argument.

JO: Yes, it's a logical consequence. And I think that's why, in some ways, the ideal state that he develops has these "strangely"—as people have pointed out—democratic features. He tries to, in some ways, do an end-run around it by saying that we can bracket these democratic features in various ways in his ideal state. But ultimately I think he has bought himself into a world in which the best possible form of public order has features of democracy—that is, we all communicate and reason together in the act of creating higher forms of public goods.

Questions for Discussion:

1. *Do you agree with Josh that Aristotle correctly identified our fundamental human capacities? Did he leave any out? Did he include something that is not really an essential attribute of our humanity?*

2. *Might there be some people who don't possess the same constitutive capacities that most others do, or have them to a different degree?*

VIII. Increasing Eudaimonia

Improving democracy

HB: So allow me to play devil's advocate again. If I look around, say, California today, I certainly see that there are lots of people who are very social. There are also some who are rational—let's say lots of people, although I'm perhaps being generous here. At any rate, they're engaging in all sorts of social activity, forms of social organization: they go to their PTA meetings, they involve themselves in their neighbourhood community center and so forth. And, as you say, they are communicating a lot with each other.

So they are certainly social animals; and they seem, more or less, to be flourishing, relatively speaking. But at the same time that they're doing all of this, they're not voting. On the whole they seem to be voting less than they used to 20 or 30 years ago. So their constitutive capacities are being met to the extent that they're not like our cat in a box—they seem to be, to the outside observer at least, living happy lives—but this doesn't seem to be manifesting itself in terms of active democratic involvement. How would you respond to that?

JO: I think that the move that you are suggesting is that we should think about being a democratic citizen as being a voter. And that, of course, would be very strange from the point of view of any Athenian or other Greek city that was democratic—or Aristotle, for that matter. They don't suppose that voting on an occasional basis for a party's candidate would be rightly understood as exercising their political capacities.

HB: Okay, fair enough. Let me rephrase my question. Same people, same state, same activities. By and large—Thomas Piketty's bestseller notwithstanding—they don't seem to be terribly preoccupied by, or frustrated with, the fact that they are largely left out of the governing process.

From the framework of our proverbial cat in a box, it is not as if their constitutive capacities seem to be terribly constrained: they seem to be flourishing in all sorts of different ways, independent of any political manifestation of these capacities.

If that's true—and perhaps that's not true, perhaps they are somehow feeling constrained and miserable in ways that I am not properly sensitive to—then it seems to me that we have a counter-example to this idea of democratic engagement being a natural consequence of these three core principles.

JO: This brings us to the question of what the nature of the community we're talking about is. Aristotle had a very clear argument about this. He thought that the city-state was the proper size, the highest form of social organization for humans. He really thought that humans are political in that they are well-designed to live in a *polis*, in a city-state. That's because he thought that if you get bigger than a polis, then you're going to have a difficult time really engaging in politics at the right level. The city-state, then, was the level of ruling, taking your part in governing the community, and then being ruled over in your turn.

Aristotle didn't think everybody should be doing politics all the time, but he thought that at some point in your life you should actively participate in what we would call engagement in governance.

So we can't say that the problem is that people don't live in city-states anymore, and that we ought to because that is central to us becoming the perfect political animal. That would be a funny kind of argument to be making.

The question is, then, if we want to use this Aristotelian frame in some way that is effective, how can we take the—for the moment, anyway—highest form of self-governing community—the nation-state—and find ways in which citizens can engage in something that is more than just voting occasionally? How can we involve them in governing, using their reasoning capacity and their communicative capacity to govern together with others?

Or do we say that the nation-state is only one example out of many possible human communities that enable people to engage in a desirable form of self-governance?

So, you make a choice. Or maybe it's both.

As we were talking about this earlier, maybe there are ways to use technology, theories of networks, social media, and so on, to think about how a national government could be more in the hands of its citizens. Maybe things could be structured in such a way that when I send a tweet or something to the White House, I feel that I've actually engaged in the kind of activity that an Athenian in the assembly regularly did, shouting with his other fellow citizens, "*Sit down, you idiot, let someone who knows what to say speak now.*"

HB: You're having a little shout.

JO: Yes. You're having a little shout. And I don't think it's ridiculous to think that we could imagine how to do that.

HB: And in fact, since I brought up California, there are various mechanisms already in place—namely referenda—where citizens *do* get more involved in governance. I'm not at all a student of this, but my sense is that this is fairly unique.

JO: The referendum exists in most of the American western states. It was a pretty common reform that really goes back to the late 19th and early 20th century, the progressive era. Then it sat fallow for a long time, until especially California, and now other states too, began using it more regularly.

So yes: there are ways in which citizens do make judgements together, but they tend to do it very badly, because we haven't really thought through how we ought to collectively engage in this kind of decision-making.

It's funny; I can walk down the corridor shortly before a California election in what can reasonably claim to be one of the best political science departments in the world, and ask my colleagues, "*What should I think about proposition 320?*"

And my colleagues, who are **really** high-end political scientists, will likely scratch their heads and say, "*I haven't a clue. I haven't read carefully enough. It's a pretty complex matter.*"

And I think to myself, *Wow, if that's true, we're not doing it right.* So we haven't thought through how to use referenda in ways that would allow citizens to actually make some kind of judgement that would be rational.

But once again, I think there are ways to think that through better as well.

My Stanford colleague Jim Fishkin has a system of bringing together groups of individuals for what he calls deliberative polls: giving them a couple of days to work together as a group on the pros and cons of various real-world decisions that have to be made. Now, they don't have legislative authority, but some of them have been taken seriously by various governments throughout the world.

HB: The idea here is to be able to capitalize on different, potentially overlapping, areas of knowledge of different people? To be able to harness this Aristotelian group social behaviour, as it were?

JO: Right. Fishkin's approach is focused on distilling true interests from mere preferences.

His idea is to study how a cross-section of the relevant voting group—say, the people of California, or whatever it may be— would choose to vote if they really had a chance to work through the issues and listen to experts on both sides of the issues, to interact with one another and hear people who are presently affected in various ways by the issue, so as to think more deeply about how they, in turn, might be affected.

In other words, if they really had a chance to deliberate—give reasons to one another, hear other people's reasons—how would they vote on specific issues?

Basically, what he does on any given topic that's the focus of one of these polls is to ask people to fill out a questionnaire beforehand about their opinions on various things relevant to the decision that has to be made. Then they go through this "treatment", as it were, of listening to experts and talking things over with each other, and at the end they fill out the same questionnaire and he measures the difference between the two.

The difference is often quite considerable across the whole group. He suggests that, if the group is truly representative of the larger group, the second set of results is the way the whole group would choose if they had time to really think it all through.

That's one part of it. The other way to think about bringing a group together and making a judgement with a group is what's sometimes called epistemic, or knowledge-based, approaches to democracy. In this case you assume different people have different information, different forms of knowledge, and different cognitive frameworks that they bring to bear on questions.

Once again, the idea is that we might come up with a better solution by aggregating these through sharing information: "*Tell me what **you** know that's relevant to the problem, and I'll tell you what **I** know*"; "*Oh, that's interesting, I hadn't thought of **that** before; here's how **I** think about those sorts of problems...*"

Fishkin's approach involves giving people an opportunity to better appreciate the settled sense of their own interest and beliefs to answer yes or no on a specific issue. The epistemic approach says that, actually, we might even ask a *better* question, or we might come up with a solution that wasn't even on the table in the first place, if only we had the chance to productively share publicly all of the things that we know individually.

Both are part and parcel of a way of understanding being a democratic citizen that's really much more robust than just occasionally going into a voting booth and choosing a representative.

HB: And this also helps us arrive at a sense of what is genuinely, as best as one can determine, in the best interests of the citizenry. This gets back to what you said before about people being forced to choose between candidates who are purporting to be speaking for their interests. By going down these paths, you are developing a probe to better understand what those interests actually are in the first place.

JO: That's right; any kind of epistemic or knowledge-based approach to democracy *does* make an assumption that there are actually better and worse solutions to problems. Therefore, there are some things that genuinely are in the collective interest of the community. Even though there may be some individuals in the community who say, "*I still reject that,*" the idea is that there really are, objectively speaking, some things that are in the interest of the community as a whole.

That's controversial in and of itself. Some approaches to democracy say that it's all about preference aggregation: just take people as given, assume that people have their own interests at heart —which they know fairly clearly—and say that the only way we can coherently keep going as a society is simply to decide where the majority of those preferences happens to lie right now. Have the vote and get on with it.

But these other approaches—represented by Aristotle and almost anybody who is interested in these deliberative or epistemic approaches to democracy—suppose that we can probably do better than just aggregating preferences. Either we can refine our preferences, and make them more like true interests, or we can come up with better solutions that actually are in the collective good.

HB: But it seems to me from what you're saying that there is a fundamental difference in kind between those who believe in preference aggregation and those who believe in something much stronger—and that you have a strong attachment to the second category.

So let me try to pin you down a little bit. If one buys this "inspired-by Aristotle" argument that you were making earlier—that our rationality, sociability, communicative skills and so forth are fundamental, constitutive aspects of our character, and that it's in the best interest of any being to be flourishing, which is to say, utilizing and harnessing these constitutive capacities—then the claim is that this necessarily leads to democracy, because otherwise you're denying people the right to partake of the sorts of interactions that are represented by these constitutive capacities.

And I would argue that this would also indicate that a system which maximizes the use of these capacities, through this deliberative process or other more complex measures, is *inherently superior* to just checking out what people's preferences are, because in the first instance you're actually enabling them to use their communicative instincts, rationality, sociability and all that as a way of forming decisions.

JO: That's exactly right. That's why the kind of democrat I am is of this epistemic sort. Yes, I buy into this whole package of, roughly speaking, Aristotelian understanding of what is good for me and you and other humans, and what is good for the collective.

I think that we will get to a better decision—we'll have "better honey", as it were, if we were bees—and we'll also have had a better time of it as individuals. It's both that you get a better outcome and you have a better life, a more flourishing life.

The whole end of life for Aristotle was *eudaimonia*, which is sometimes called happiness or flourishing. It's not happiness like feeling pleasure all the time, it means having lived your life as fully as possible in pursuing the kind of being that you are.

HB: A psychologist might call it "self-actualization".

JO: Yes, that's right. And it's not the kind of self-actualization that says, "*I should just be number one.*" There are cheap ways to do self-actualization.

But this is simply to say, "*What am I? I am a certain kind of animal, so how ought I to live my life so that I might be the best of that sort of being possible?*"

If you have done that through the course of a life, then Aristotle says that you had a flourishing life. That's the most you could hope for. And that's a lot.

For him, that's pretty much everything.

Questions for Discussion:

1. Do you think that some version of "deliberative democracy" will ever supplant our standard representational democracy?

2. To what extent can we be certain that most representational democratic structures actually reveal what people's preferences are? To what extent can we be certain that most people know what their own preferences really are?

3. What role does education play in the development of an enhanced form of democracy? Do most people have sufficient skills to critically examine a policy issue even if they had a more comprehensive opportunity to do so?

IX. Dignity

An essential ingredient of a flourishing democracy

HB: I'd like to talk about the concept of dignity, which is something else I know you feel strongly about. Because improving our structures is not just about one's own self-actualization and flourishing, important though that may be. It also has repercussions on how you treat other people and how you interact with others.

JO: Yes. You tend to think about the two big democratic values as being equality and freedom. That's fine. That's a great place to start, as far as I'm concerned. If we're free and equal—at least politically free and politically equal—we're doing pretty well.

The third value, dignity, sometimes gets sort of "outsourced" to what is thought of as purely human rights language, and therefore is not strictly considered a part of democracy but rather as part of something that would stand "above" democracy as a kind of basic human right.

I'm all for human rights, of course; and it's certainly true that a human life does not go as well as it ought to in the absence of dignity. But I also think that dignity is a natural part of a democratic community, because dignity that is *only* a "human right", independent of a civic community that is sustaining it through the chosen actions of the members of that community, is not likely to actually be preserved.

So, what is dignity, anyway? There are lots of ways to think about it. The way I think about it is pretty simplistic: to be dignified means to be a sharer in equal high standing in your community. You should have a standing that is in some ways equal. Your standing as a citizen, as an individual, is equal to that of others—and it's high. It's not equally miserable. It's equally elevated.

That means, practically speaking, that you live without fear, without the experience of humiliation and without the fear or experience of infantilization. It means that the other people in your community do not seek to subject you to humiliation, and they don't treat you as less of an adult than you are. It's fine to treat an infant in an infantilizing way, but not good to treat an adult in an infantilizing way.

These aren't meant to be terribly technical definitions, and everyone can pull out of their own experience what they think it means to be humiliated, or what it is to be infantilized. It's also not meant to be cheapened down to something like, *I oughtn't ever be affronted* or *I oughtn't ever be made to feel uncomfortable*. Humiliation has to be stronger than that. It has to in some way imply being treated in a way that you are not a possessor of equal high standing with others in your community.

The basic thought is that if you are free and equal and you get to live a dignified life, then you have the basic framework that you need to be a democratic citizen. I also think that these are just basic goods: that we have reasons to want to be free, equal and live without humiliation and infantilization that stand *outside* of this whole democratic story.

In my work on this, I say that if you don't grasp that, if you say, *"Well, no, actually, I think it's fine to humiliate and infantilize people—I do it all the time and I rather enjoy it,"* or *"Actually, I quite like being humiliated,"* I'm left without any suitable response. But I'm pretty convinced that that's not the case for most of us.

HB: So I won't try to make that argument, you'll perhaps be relieved to know. I'm going to say something else. I see how ensuring this high level of dignity certainly enables and facilitates the democratization process, but does it work the other way? Is the existence of a universally high level of dignity a natural consequence of a real democracy?

JO: I think it is, insofar as I think that you can't have a democracy without this. Imagine that you're perfectly free to come to the assembly—there are no bullies who are going to officially bar you admittance—and you have an equal right to speak in the assembly, but you also know that the people who are the important people in the society are going to laugh and sneer and do their best to humiliate you in every possible way that they can whenever you try to say something. Are you going to come to the assembly? No, of course you're not going to. You don't want to suffer humiliation.

You'll feel that sort of prior restraint. In some ways, then, dignity is the thing that makes real your free and equal opportunity to participate, ensuring that what you say in public is taken seriously to the extent to which it deserves to be taken seriously.

Now if I go into a meeting of theoretical physicists and say, "*Well, I'm a free and equal person, and I'm also dignified, so I'd like to tell you guys a few things about my opinions on string theory,*" they'd say, "*Sit down, you silly man.*"

HB: Most likely. But then, they say that to everyone.

JO: Maybe so. But the point, of course, is that it's not just that I have the right to feel fine about myself no matter what sort of silly thing I do.

But, once again, if I'm in a political forum in which I have something to say, or some reason to think I have something to contribute, I ought to be attended to with a sort of seriousness, instead of being told, "*You're from the wrong part of the country,*" or "*You have a funny accent,*" or "*You're the wrong colour,*" or all the various reasons that people might think that it would be a good idea for me to be humiliated instead of taken seriously.

HB: So a proper democratic structure necessarily entails a minimal, maybe even robust, level of dignity at some universal level.

JO: Yes, I think so. And it means that we have to be willing to act in defense of one another's dignity, because in every society there are those who like humiliating others. The Greeks certainly realized that: they had a whole vocabulary for it.

We've probably each met people like that, people for whom part of the pleasure in life involves lowering other people in one way or another—making them feel bad or treating them in an infantile way. Those people need to be resisted. If we don't collectively resist them, if we don't act in defense of the dignity of each and every one of us, then we're going to get a cascade of indignity that will ultimately, I think, tear down the structure of democracy. Or just leave a shell.

It really is a problem of collective action, because often standing up against bullies, especially when they're bullying somebody else, takes a certain kind of courage. But it doesn't take superhuman courage if you believe that other people are going to stand with you against that bully. If I say, "*That's wrong, don't speak to her like that,*" and if I know that my fellow citizens will stand with me and say, "*He's right, that's wrong,*" then I don't have to be exceptionally brave.

Aristotle has a whole theory of virtues, and courage is one of them. But the point is that it doesn't take any special kind of courage if I come to believe that standing up to a bully will be recognized and reinforced by others in my community rather than leaving me isolated. In other words, standing up to the bully requires a mechanism that we can collectively act together against these kinds of actions.

This is one way to think about what hate speech laws do, to take one example. People like hate speech laws or don't like them, but their existence is an example of the law serving as a bright line. When somebody uses something that is recognized as hate speech, I can say, "*Ah, they have crossed the line.*" The line is meant to avoid the humiliation of people. Therefore I ought to, as a law-abiding citizen, say something when I've encountered an example of hate speech. I ought to say, "*Stop, I'll report you.*"

There are various ways to imagine both formal rules, like hate speech laws, but also social conventions—*We don't do that around here. That's not the way we talk to each other around here*—as triggers that yield a collective response. That way, in a properly functioning society as I imagine it, there is the assent of the community such that the bully is then dissuaded.

HB: Right. There's obviously a private sense of morality—we all like to believe that we have a handle on what is wrong and right and that people should act in a moral way—but there's also this notion of pro-actively following a certain course in order to ensure proper governing policy, the well-structuring of society.

There's a societal, communal, motivation that should be part and parcel of any well-governed, responsible society.

JO: That's right. And it's not just altruistic. If I don't stand up to say something to this bully who is bullying you, *I* might well be next. Or if I'm not next, maybe I'm going to be third in line, or something like that. But I can perfectly well foresee a society in which, if bullies get to do what they like and humiliate whomever they want, then eventually I'm going to be a victim too.

So by acting pro-actively now, I am not only doing the right thing, I'm also acting in my own core interest: I want to do it *now* before *I'm* the victim.

It's a way in which the ethical impulse to do the right thing can also be related to a perfectly self-interested impulse of not wanting to have my own life degraded, not having a less flourishing existence than I might otherwise have.

Questions for Discussion:

1. Can dignity be revoked? Are there some people who, through their actions, don't deserve to be treated with dignity? If so, what does that imply for how society should consider them politically, according to Josh?

2. Will a blatantly disrespectful top-level politician necessarily cause a disproportionate amount of damage to a democracy? If so, what does this imply about the importance of choosing political leaders who conscientiously exhibit a sense of dignity?

3. To what extent is dignity related to empathy?

X. Keeping It Real

Engaging the general public with scholarly insights

HB: So now it's time to make a lateral move to the guy on the street reading this, who might say something like, "*Okay, this Ober fellow seems like a very smart guy who has a lot of things figured out. He's a serious scholar who's been able to make fundamental and insightful connections between our current political structure and ancient Athenian democracy, and I'll even grant that his work has some direct implications for my life. But how are his thoughts going to have impact? He's in a political science department at Stanford. That's all very nice: they hold conferences and write papers. They have tea. At some point, perhaps, they will discuss amongst themselves the various propositions in play on a California referendum, and recognize that they don't have much deeper insights than I do. Scholarship is all well and good, but if what you're saying is true, and the stakes are as high as we're talking about, then that should somehow be able to be communicated into the body politic, it should somehow be able to directly affect society.*"

Put more succinctly, how would you respond to the question, *How do your thoughts and those of your colleagues map on to concretely changing society for the better?*

JO: I don't have a great answer to that, because I think that there really is a place in the society for public intellectuals who have a big public voice—those who write regularly for major media, and who have hundreds of thousands of Twitter followers and so on and so forth. And I think that there's also a place in society for people who work at the fundamental level of either values or science.

There are not very many people, I think, who do both of those things really well. Personally, I don't think I do the first thing particularly well. As for the second, well, I'm talking with you...

HB: It's working for me.

JO: I'm happy to try to engage outside of the world of my fellow academics. But I think that being able to really reach out in a big way and put ideas in a sharp, accessible and powerful idiom that can capture a lot of attention is a somewhat different skill than most academics have.

I think what universities are supposed to be for is generating ideas and making them accessible enough so that those who *do* have the skills to create a big voice, a big following, can embrace them—should they choose to—and get access to them.

Once again, Thomas Piketty's work is a great example of this. His thoughts have been amplified and sharpened for a mass audience in all kinds of ways. As you said earlier, lots and lots of people bought the book. Probably not as many read it page by page, but a lot of people would nonetheless be able to give you the basic argument of the book because of the ways in which it's been taken up by the media.

I suppose the basic point is that universities—and other places where people do fundamental work on values and on science— need to be the kind of places that can connect to this. It's not right to just sit back and say, "*I live in an ivory tower and have no interest in ever even knowing that these other people exist. I write for my peers in political science or classics and those are the only people I care about.*" If I act that way, I haven't done what I should be doing. I should be at least *trying* to make what I do accessible.

On the other hand, the notion that every academic doing basic research should also be a public intellectual—that I should necessarily be out there pushing a Twitter account—is false. I think that it confuses the idea that both of these are really valuable things to do—

HB: And that it's necessarily the case that everybody should do both.

JO: Right. So that's a blurry idea, but I think it's really at the point of how to design a university. If I'm running this university, what kind of incentives do I give my faculty or graduate students or other members of the university community to communicate with others?

If I say, *"Look, the higher you get in the ranks of the faculty, the less you'll have to teach those miserable undergraduates, because what do they really know? You'll only have to teach graduates, and only the best of the graduates, and maybe not even them,"* then maybe the university hasn't been optimally designed.

Because people who are doing fundamental research really *should* be out there talking to first-year students, trying to communicate what they know and what they do research on, to reach—at least in that sense—a broader audience. And I think good universities do exactly that.

HB: While ensuring that the faculty are themselves challenged by the students.

JO: That's right, exactly. I think that there are always tendencies in universities to go in different directions, in terms of what the incentives and rules are—there's always the danger of disappearing into that highest chamber of the ivory tower and communicating only with your fellow residents of that highest chamber.

But, once again, I believe that great universities push against that tendency. They say, *"After all, no matter how great a scholar you are, part of your job is to disseminate what you know, at least to our students, and maybe to our alumni, and maybe to some extent to the wider world in one way or another."*

HB: Right. Anything I missed? Anything you want to add?

JO: I don't think so. It's been a great conversation for me. I'm always really happy to talk about the world of the ancients, not only in terms of why it's just terrifically interesting in and of itself, but especially if we can relate it to things that citizens in a modern society ought to be thinking about—and sometimes, in fact, **are** thinking about, but perhaps aren't generally encouraged to think about as deeply or carefully or passionately as maybe they ought.

HB: Well, you've helped a lot. Thanks a lot, Josh.

JO: Thanks very much.

Questions for Discussion:

1. Do universities generally do a good enough job at providing vehicles for researchers like Josh to engage with the general public? If not, what steps could they take to improve the situation?

2. Under what circumstances should a member of the general public be more sceptical of the academic who is anxious to appear on television as a pundit than one who is reluctant to do so?

3. Is the phrase "public intellectual" a meaningful one in contemporary society? To what extent does the desire to become a "public intellectual" imply a disproportionate concern for being an authority rather than being a well-recognized scholar?

Continuing the Conversation

Readers passionate about the topic of this conversation are referred to Josh's many other books on this subject: *Demokratia: A Conversation on Democracies, Ancient and Modern, The Rise and Fall of Classical Greece, Demopolis: Democracy before Liberalism in Theory and Practice, Democracy and Knowledge: Innovation and Learning in Classical Athens* and *Political Dissent in Democratic Athens: Intellectual Critics of Popular Rule.*

Democracy

Clarifying the Muddle

A conversation with John Dunn

Introduction

Democratic Daze

Democracy confuses me. It always has.

Pericles spoke about it in emphatically glowingly terms: much more than just a particular form of rule, to him it was nothing less than a triumphant demonstration of Athenian moral superiority.

Then, for more than two millennia, it largely disappeared off the face of the earth, universally regarded by virtually all sophisticated political figures (very much including, as it happens, the vast majority of the Founding Fathers of the United States) as utopian, unrealizable and downright dangerous—a recipe for the worst sort of government possible: populist, short-termist and deeply irrational.

Then, against all odds, democracy suddenly became the only game in town, nothing less than the hallmark of a civilized society, even invoked as a cause worth going to war for to defend or promote.

But what does it *mean*, exactly?

Not, surely, that governments must act according to the rule of law. Or even, for that matter, to determine what those laws must be. For those things, logically, are quite unconnected to what democracy properly is.

One could certainly imagine, for example, a monarchy embracing a Universal Declaration of Human Rights (as sometimes occurs) or a democracy egregiously violating it (as often occurs).

And, just as surely, the message is hardly that all citizens of democracies will regularly have a role to play in the affairs of the state. That sort of democracy hasn't really existed since Alexander the Great put an end to it in ancient Athens.

Like most people reading this, I grew up in a representative democracy—which simply meant that once every four or five years or so I had the privilege of trudging down to the local polling booth to tick off a particular box on a piece of paper that, when combined with those of my fellow box-tickers, produced a "political result" that was swiftly interpreted by a bevy of vigorous spin-doctors as some sort of "clear mandate" for whatever the winner judged most convenient.

I was never asked to make a judgment on any particular economic policy. I never weighed in on the merits of any social program. Indeed, I've never voted on any piece of legislation whatsoever. The sum total of my "democratic responsibilities" lay in ticking off a box a few times per decade.

Quite frankly it's pretty hard for me to regard any of this as a great cause for pride or celebration. Our form of democracy seems to work, more or less, or at least not often result in a complete disaster, which often amounts to the same thing for the great majority of us who don't spend too much time delving deeply into the nuances of political theory and governance.

But for those who *are* so inclined, there is clearly a great deal more to say. Take John Dunn. A deeply incisive and wide-ranging scholar, John has written widely on revolution, regime collapse and reconstruction and the history of political thought.

Most recently, however, he's been diligently investigating the history, current development and future of democracy, penning such works as *Setting the People Free: The Story of Democracy* and *Breaking*

Democracy's Spell in an effort to not only rigorously describe how we got to our present state, but also to explode the many hyperbolic distortions and false claims that still so often accompany the word "democracy" in the public consciousness.

And while his cool, objective analysis is inevitably portrayed by his critics as that of a stuffy, reactionary elitist, the truth is very different indeed. Consistently concerned with how to achieve genuine political and social progress, he is neither "pro" nor "anti" democracy, but—much more importantly—simply a deeply knowledgeable scholar who dares to take a critical scalpel to our current political systems and carefully point out when the many often hyperinflated declarations we are bombarded with are simply false.

Of course, sometimes they're true. One principal achievement of the Indian experience of democracy, he told me, was the weakening of a repressive caste structure through the advent of its democratic practices.

> *"That is a very considerable achievement politically, and I think that it is owed to democracy. It isn't owed just to the idea of democracy, but it's owed to the extent to which the idea of democracy has been realized, at least through the electoral structure in India."*

After all John insists, the object of the game isn't about categorization systems or who gets the credit. It's simply about results.

> *"The point of political institutions isn't to look good; the point of political institutions is to have good consequences."*

And the best way to create good consequences, according to John, is to genuinely increase our political understanding so that we can begin to change our societies for the better.

> *"If you don't understand politics, you can't have any coherent conception of how the immense damage that human beings have done to the planet on which they live can be brought under even minimal control within the foreseeable future. And if it isn't brought under*

control, then there almost certainly won't be good human lives in a few hundred years; there just won't be able to be."

That should certainly get the attention of anyone who thought that this was just some abstruse, academic discussion. Political understanding hits us where we live. But how do we actually go about developing it?

Well, an obvious place to turn to would be experts in the discipline of political science. After all, offering well-informed judgments on politics should presumably be their day job.

But according to John, most political scientists are a long way from providing any measure of real support to the rest of us.

"Most academics who work on political theory, political philosophy, or political sociology, concentrate on what they think are well-defined questions. And they believe that they provide robust and compelling answers to these well-defined questions.

"Now, in order to be able to do that with political stuff, you have to pull a long way back from the world. And my general intuitive judgment is that, if you pull a long way back from the world of politics, you just lose politics. It's gone. Politics is in the dynamism and unobviousness of what is actually there. It's in the chaotic character of human interaction.

"So if you ask, 'Who needs political science departments?' the answer isn't clear Obviously political scientists need political science departments, but it isn't unequivocally clear that anyone else actually needs them.

"Nobody tries to answer what, after all, in the end is the primary question, which is, 'What the hell is really going on and why is it going on?'"

Harsh words? Perhaps. But in order to get the clearest grasp of what's actually going on around us, harsh words are often just the ticket, if only to jolt us out of our preconceived notions and assumptions.

And John Dunn, an internationally renowned political thinker of the highest order, is quite willing to provide them.

The Conversation

I. Illusions and Confusions

Unmasking American stereotypes

HB: You've been talking and writing about democracy for some time; and in your book, *Breaking Democracy's Spell*, you discuss such notions as "the spell of democracy" and "the veil of democracy". What are you talking about here, exactly, and why is this an important thing to be concerned with?

JD: Well, it's an important thing to be concerned with because democracy as a word and an idea has a unique political force in the world. And an awful lot of people's political responses are in the end organized in one way or another in response to its presence.

I got interested in it pretty accidentally—it wasn't because I had some special insight—but I've spent a lot of time thinking about it and trying to understand what's been happening in it. And I think I've understood something very important about it that isn't generally understood: namely, how it's come about that it's so prominent and that it has the sort of effect it does have on people's political comprehension.

People can only understand politics through ideas: they can't understand it just by *looking* or *smelling*. And the ideas through which they try to understand it mostly don't help very much. In fact, very many of these ideas actively *impede* understanding politics—and, in fact, are *meant* to impede understanding of it.

HB: But if I'm an American sitting here listening to this, I might say, *"Well, I know what democracy is, and I know democracy is an important thing. It's what my republic is based on."*

I might even think that it was a motivating force in the generation of my republic, but at any rate I'm likely convinced that it's the right way to do politics and the model through which we should enlighten the rest of the world. That's a fairly common view, I think, that your average American would have: that we should export democracy to the rest of the world, that we should encourage other people to be democratic.

And my reaction to you might be some combination of bemusement and hostility: *"What's **your** problem, exactly, Professor Dunn? Are you an anti-democrat, somehow? You don't believe in democracy? What is all this talk about 'breaking the spell of democracy', trying to change my views? Why should I pay attention to all of that?"*

JD: Well, you should pay attention to it because your views are wrong.

That's the best reason for paying attention to someone, if your views are what's in question. I don't think that I can show you exactly *what* the right views for you are, because that depends a lot on you, and what you're actually concerned with, and very complicated judgments about the world that you shouldn't take on trust from me or anyone else.

But what is *definitely* true is that the way Americans think about democracy is very, very grievously mistaken, and it's mistaken in a number of different ways.

First of all, it isn't true, historically, the story you've just recited to me. It isn't true that the American Republic was founded on the idea of democracy. The American founders were extremely *sceptical* of democracy, and they thought it referred to a very *bad* form of government. And they very actively and militantly argued against allowing anything that would appropriately be described with that word to operate in the United States.

There are one or two momentary exceptions—the most striking of which was something that Alexander Hamilton once said. Alexander Hamilton is normally regarded by American historians as the most spectacularly antidemocratic political agent and political thinker in the history of the United States and someone who built the United States as a state that had all the wrong purposes for it to be a democracy, because a democracy in that sense is a soft responsive structure that cares for everyone equally, and it's liable to be paralyzed because of its cares and not to be very effective at doing anything.

Alexander Hamilton started off in the opposite direction, really. He began with the question of how to make the United States into a strong enough state to actually protect itself and thrive in a world in which it will very often be living with what are, essentially, competitors and enemies. And the United States that emerged—a United States which for a time was very clearly the most powerful state in the world and is still the most powerful state in the world by a sort of receding margin for a variety of reasons—the United States that came about was the sort of state, very broadly speaking, that Hamilton had in mind, and not at all the sort of state that some of the other founders had in mind.

But Hamilton did, at one point, call the United States that he was attempting to generate "a representative democracy". He didn't call it that in the context of arguments about what it *should* be like. He just used the phrase. And a lot of what is said by the most intellectually powerful and politically influential founders about democracy is straightforwardly *dis*praised.

HB: And if you look at something like the Electoral College, for example, which comes into prominence every so often when there is the spectre of a presidential candidate winning the Electoral College vote without winning the popular vote, that should trigger an acknowledgement of the fact that the founders framed a system that was not manifestly democratic.

JD: Well, it was intended to prevent certain bad things from happening which democracy as a political form was believed to make particularly likely, or even completely inevitable. So you can see it's a muddled way to think about the relationship between what those people were trying to do and democracy to say that the United States

Republic was built as a democracy and to be a democracy. It just wasn't.

What, I think, is very important about American political beliefs about this word is that those beliefs are based on the idea that there is *one* correct way to understand democracy—which is the way Americans understand democracy and the way in which their own political institutions are structured—and that these specific political institutions are, in principle, the correct ones for everyone.

Now that's certainly not what the idea of democracy means in any coherent understanding of its historical trajectory or of what the idea itself could possibly mean.

The idea couldn't possibly mean, *The Americans have a way of doing something which is the way for everyone to do it, irrespective of how everyone else thinks and feels and believes.*

The fundamental concept of democracy means that, in any place where it applies, what will be true is that the people of that place decide what they want and can be guaranteed that that will be what happens.

That's a very demanding idea. It doesn't plausibly get realized anywhere ever; but it's less obviously false in some settings at some times than it is in others at other times.

Take an important recent example. If you look at Gaza, the Gaza bit of Palestine, the most striking single example of a democratic choice was the victory of a political party or a religious movement or both, which was a catastrophic outcome from the point of view of American interest; and, presumptively, from the majority Israeli point of view—a terrible threat to the future of Israel.

There is no doubt whatever that this particular political and religious organization won that election. It didn't satisfy conditions for being a free choice and with open deliberation, or anything like that, but it certainly was the body that more people wished to win, and that's why it did win. Democracy says that should be the outcome.

So it's simply not true that the Americans have the uniquely canonical understanding of this idea, which is transparent to them, and which should be shared by everyone.

Questions for Discussion:

1. To what extent is the Electoral College system antidemocratic?

2. Are you surprised by the idea that many of America's Founding Fathers were not advocates of democracy? What sort of "bad things" do you think that they were worried about happening to the United States under a strictly democratic form of governance?

II. Historical Examinations

The power of etymology

HB: And, of course, democracy is hardly an American idea. While most people unhesitatingly focus on the ancient Athenians as soon as the topic comes up, you make it very clear in your work that historically democracy has meant very different things at very different times and one has to constantly be on one's guard against superficial interpretations and pat phrases to get a grasp of how this particular word and the concepts behind it have achieved some measure of ascendancy. In particular, you look carefully at the etymology of the word democracy and how it has evolved. Why do you do that?

JD: Well, it's because you can follow a word very, very precisely. You can go wherever the word has been and left traces and you can see it, and you can look at what was happening in and through it. What that word refers to, mind you, you can't see in quite the same way: you have to work it out.

And actually, it's quite difficult to work it out—you can begin to work it out if you pay close attention, but you can never be quite sure you've got it right. But the goal is to follow the word and try to understand what is happening with it. And if you do, you find something that is quite surprising to most people today.

As a result of a particular set of imaginative and practical shifts in the world over the last 250 years or so, one of the forms of government as they were understood in the ancient world has been a very much more successful political competitor than the other two.

There were basically three basic forms of government.

First of all, there was government by the demos, which didn't actually mean everyone—in fact, in the ancient world, it *never* meant everyone and always excluded lots and lots of people whom the previous governing class thought poorly of.

At any rate, the idea of the demos, the people, the citizens: that was an idea that could be opened very widely. And the point of it was to oppose it to the other two forms of government. It was a contrast idea.

These other two forms of government were monarchy (usually sufficiently disrecommended so as to come out as the unpleasant and destructive rule of a single person—tyranny as the Greeks called it—another word which has stuck around) and aristocracy, which meant the rule of those who were entitled to look down on most people, and unimpededly do what they wanted because they were so obviously superior.

In the course of the last 250 years or so, democracy has been a very much more successful political competitor than those other two forms.

And it's very easy to see why: it appeals to more people and is wide open to all comers, while the other two are meant to be—and obviously, in, fact were—closed against most comers.

So it wasn't surprising that the battle in the end came out that way, but it didn't come out that way until relatively recently, historically. And during the long period of time before, there weren't very many passages of European history anywhere at all in which democracy as a way of thinking about what a political regime should be was the prevalent political and social form.

It took some transformations in economic organization to make it possible that was structured according to the idea of being open to all to be established, secured and perpetuated.

Today, in a lot of places in the world, we have political forms that purport to be structures in which all adults have equal power and the political outcome and governmental processes are chosen and controlled by everyone equally.

Now, that isn't even *vaguely* true of anywhere. And it doesn't take a lot of attention to what's going on anywhere in the world to see how far from the truth it is.

But the term "democracy", which means that that's what *should* be true, has been the term that won the competition between ideas of how politics should be shaped. And the term has been institutionalized and interpreted over the last 250 years or so, and increasingly over the last 75 years or so since the Second World War.

There were extremely few places in the world that looked at all liked democracies in 1914, while between 1918 and 1939, what was going on throughout different bits of Europe was democracy failing and foundering—going under to various forms of tyranny, some of them with quite a high degree of popular support. Of course, there's a lot of political equivocation about this.

Hitler was very explicitly antidemocratic, but actually the Nazis claimed to be the representatives of the German people, to be speaking for the German people. What's "the German people"?

Well, it's the German for "demos". So it's not as though even the more "popular" tyrannies—popular for a while, anyway—that did enjoy a certain kind of majority support were enemies of the idea that political power should be organized for an entire group of people.

Democracy is that very idea, an idea whose project has very wide appeal, although realizing the project is a pretty forlorn enterprise.

In my view, you should think of democracy as an idea, as a way of interrogating what the political life of your own society is actually like—what is really happening in it, how far away it is from that particular picture of how things should be, and what it is, exactly, that causes it to be so far away.

That is a very powerful way of inquiring into the political reality of your own society, and it's a way that is open to very deep critical elaboration. So it can serve people very well, but it can only do so if they actually *use* it to do that. And to use it to do that they have to understand what is packed inside that word and that idea.

Questions for Discussion:

1. *Do you agree with John when he says that there is "nowhere where everyone has equal power and political outcomes and government processes are chosen and controlled by everyone equally"? If not, where are those places?*

2. *What does John mean, exactly, by "using democracy to interrogate what the political life of your own society is actually like"?*

III. Thinking Deeper

Minimizing political bads

HB: This brings out two points. There is the potential peril of democracy reducing to mob rule—the so-called tyranny of the majority. You mentioned Hitler and the will of the people as a possible example. One can have a political system that faithfully represents the will of the majority of people and still does all sorts of horribly egregious things. So there is the point that upholding the will of the people does not necessarily imply that there is good governance or moral governance or just governance or anything like that.

But there is something else, I think. One of the things which has long frustrated me, and I'm sure many others, is this strange conflation of "democracy"—a method for how we govern ourselves—with other things that are quite logically independent of it.

If you listen to the word democracy being thrown around on the radio or television, there is an understanding that it also somehow necessarily incorporates a number of other things: the rule of law, capitalism, free markets and so forth.

And as you have pointed out in your writings, these things are quite distinct. The way one decides to choose one's rulers does not logically have anything to do with whether the rule of law is upheld in one's society. It does not logically entail a particular economic system. But nowadays all of these words, or at least all of these connotations, seem to come out when you utter the word "democracy", which makes everything even more of a muddle.

JD: Yes, I think that's all true. And I think it's particularly, conspicuously and disastrously true in the American rendering of things, because it's true that Americans find it extremely difficult to believe that the idea of democracy isn't somehow or other very tightly connected indeed with the idea of the rule of law, very tightly indeed connected with the idea of civil liberties, and very tightly indeed connected with the institutional structures of a capitalist society.

And they view those structures in a very uncritical and very obtuse way: they don't understand the structures to any significant degree. So they conflate things that are actually very often fairly close to being straightforwardly contradictory. It's not just that they don't go adhesively together. Actually, they don't go together *at all*.

The idea that you could have a world of political equals that was also a world of very, very drastic economical un-equals doesn't make causal sense. It can't be true. There *can't* be such a world. And there jolly well isn't.

And the idea that there is a guarantee of civil liberties in doing what the majority of a population wants done at a particular time is nothing less than incoherent. Civil liberties, if they are guaranteed by a legal structure and by a constitutional order, are guaranteed by their potential robustness *in the face of* whatever the current political preferences are. So these ideas just don't fit together.

HB: Such guarantees concern freedom from persecution for minorities—safeguards to ensure that people who might have a dissenting view or consider themselves culturally distinct from the majority are able to represent themselves exactly as a member of that majority would.

JD: Yes. I think that the key point is that there is a very large number of potential political bads. Many of the political bads can be understood very easily, and all of these ideas we've been discussing here are, in a way, strategies against particular political bads.

But actually, there can't be one structure that guarantees against all political bads. If you think that there might be then you've just lost the plot. You just have no picture of what the world is like or could be like—your thinking doesn't make any sense at all.

That's important to the way I try to think about these things, because I believe people would be, in some deep and steady sense, significantly better off if they better understood what was going on.

You may think that isn't true. And there have been very powerful political defenses of just the right distribution of ignorance and impotence: the ignorance of those who disagree with our picture and the impotence of those who might obstruct realizing it.

But I disagree. I think it is a *good* thing for power to be more equally distributed amongst human beings because human beings are potentially very dangerous to one another: they're of severely limited imaginative sympathy with one another and they are of at least equally limited generosity towards one another.

Most people can be generous to a few people, and most people have some glimmerings of comprehension of some other people, but we don't, and can't, understand other people *en gros*, so we can't really know anything about them: we can't see them and we can't begin to fathom what's really going on with them. And we don't really care, anyway.

So it doesn't make sense to trust all other human beings to be your friend and to care for you and to know how to care for you. It doesn't make any sense at all.

In that sense democracy represents the idea that almost everyone—save, perhaps the very powerful people—would be very much safer if they had a better understanding of *what* is going on and *why* it is going on.

Questions for Discussion:

1. How do modern societies safeguard against "the tyranny of the majority"? To what extent do you think they do this successfully?

2. Is a certain amount of wealth inequality necessary for any "free society"?

IV. Trust and Belief

Thinking critically

HB: So, we can't tar you with the elitist brush, then: that you're someone who is opposed to democracy in principle because you don't believe that the people should be trusted to make the right decisions.

JD: Let me just say one thing about that, because this is a very classical point. I believe that people who rule are generally not good candidates for being trusted, and that how trustworthy they are matters very much more than how trustworthy most of the rest of us are.

This is an important political point, which is very memorably expressed by John Locke, about the idiocy of putting yourself completely at the mercy of people whose purposes you have no reason whatever to trust.

That's a very strong political point. If you take that political point and run with it, you might end up with an idea rather like democracy. You wouldn't end up with the view that it was a very effective safety guarantee, because there *aren't* any very effective safety guarantees, but you'd end up with the thought that that's more the right sort of shape, politically.

HB: Of course, Churchill had this famous line that democracy is the worst form of government other than all the others that have been tried from time to time.

But I do want to get back for a moment to this notion of the strident American we've been picking on, this naive American who has unthinkingly conflated all sorts of different and logically independent ideas with that of democracy, who is triumphantly talking about exporting "American-style democracy" around the world and so forth. I think that perhaps we should temper that with another point that you've made in your books and lectures.

You mentioned that there seems to be some weird sort of dichotomy that actually happens within the American body politic, or even the average American on the street, which is this notion that alongside this naively triumphant view that, *We have the recipe for how society should be structured and we should engage in the American mission of exporting our democracy to enlighten the rest of the world*, is the reality that many Americans are actually very sophisticated and very critical of the shortcomings and failures of their own political system. They certainly don't routinely claim that their leaders are invariably astute, morally upstanding, individuals of great probity.

And so there is almost this bipolar nature to them: when they look at themselves they can be very critical, very astute, very sensitive to transgressions and certainly don't imagine that they're living in some panacea, but at the same time they're able to actually think quite naively and superficially about both "exporting democracy" and the intrinsic superiority of their country.

Is this strange combination of sophistication and naivety something particular to the economic success of the American experiment, you think, or is this something that is reflective of a more universal aspect of the human condition?

JD: I think it's quite possible that any state that was very, very powerful, had been very powerful for quite a long time, and had been very little threatened from the outside would become overconfident about its own merits.

I think it's perfectly possible that within 50 years' time the Chinese will have as distorted and objectionable a picture of their own political system as the Americans do now. I don't think many of them really think that now, but it might be true that in 50 years' time. If China does very well economically, it might be true that they'll simply think that they've always been the most civilized place in the world, and that they've always known, more or less, how to do things properly.

And they may well end up, if that happens, addressing the world with the same sort of arrogance, and, in turn, incomprehension of political reality, that many Americans now exhibit.

Questions for Discussion:

1. Do you think that the characterization of "the average American" in this chapter and other chapters is fair and accurate?

2. What role do you think that "soft power"—movies, television, pop music and so forth—has played in American self-confidence?

V. China

Challenging Western ideals?

HB: Do you think that the rapid economic rise of China will cause Americans to second-guess their naive, triumphalist view of their own society?

JD: Well, I don't think it does, yet. It certainly causes lots of Americans much anxiety about their economic future. And how optimistic you are about that depends quite a lot on your degree of ideological self-confidence, because if your degree of ideological self-confidence is not very high and you have to derive your expectations from what's been happening to the United States as a political structure interacting with its economy for the last ten years or so, you need to be very sanguine indeed.

You need to have a very robust temperament, because it doesn't look to me as though the relationship between the United States' political processes—let's call them democratic, since Americans do—and the United States' economic functioning, is going at all well. And it doesn't look or feel to the great majority of the American population as though it is going at all well either.

It looks pretty good if you look at it from right at the top. It looks pretty ghastly if you look at it from right at the bottom—well, most states look pretty ghastly if you look at them right from the bottom—but it has shifted very sharply from a shape in which quite a large proportion of America's population felt that their economic position had improved substantially over decades to one in which quite a large proportion recognize that that is no longer the case.

HB: You make this interesting point in many of your books when you emphasize the distinction between the process of how one chooses one's rulers and whether or not one has been effectively ruled and effectively governed.

You say, *"Let's compare what has happened in the United States since 1979 to the present day to what has happened in China since 1979 to the present day."*

Clearly the rulers of the two states were decided upon in a very, very different process, and yet if you were to try to determine whether or not the average American has a relatively superior standard of living today compared to what he had in 1979, it's not so clear what the answer would be. But it's unequivocally clear what the answer would be for the vast majority of Chinese.

And so there's an objective case that could be made, independent of any other considerations, that China has been better governed, or at least relatively better governed from an economic perspective, than the United States has been over that same time period.

JD: Well, I think that's true. I think it's very difficult to tell how well a country has been governed from an economic point of view except retrospectively.

There certainly are very drastic instabilities in the Chinese process with respect to, say, the formidable environmental and ecological costs in the way it's being done—as there were, actually, in the United States when it was being done there—but it is just true that the daily living conditions of a very large proportion of the Chinese population have changed very dramatically indeed. There might have been one or two instances in history where the pace of change has been as fast as that, but certainly nothing on anything vaguely resembling that sort of scale. So the number of human lives that have been transformed by this change is very much larger than anything that has happened before.

Meanwhile, you can say, *"The United States has pursued many other admirable purposes in this time and has had some success in pursuing some of them."* You have to be rather careful which ones you pick, but you could almost certainly say the United States' record on civil rights is superior to that of China.

There is plenty of stuff on the other side of the balance: after all, the United States was a slave society. China wasn't really a slave society. There were some slaves here and there at different times, but it wasn't really a slave society. The United States, though, *was* a slave society. That's not too good from a civil rights point of view. And the aftermath of it has never been very good either.

A great deal of what's happening now you can think of as the aftermath, including the ethnic composition of today's prison population in the United States. You have to have a very feeble conception of civil rights to think that these are actually realized for a very large number of Americans.

HB: OK, but let's stick to economic matters for the moment. And when you're trying to move forwards with the largest economic transformation in the history of mankind for which there is no particular road map, the obvious question is whether or not the best possible job has been done.

As you said, the point is to be able to look at that on its own terms: to ask, *Were the right decisions actually made? Were the right policies invoked? Did we move forwards in the most coherent way we could have possibly imagined doing?* and *What lessons can we can learn from that?* without necessarily conflating this with the process of how the leaders were chosen to begin with, not only because these are actually two different things, but also because, to some extent, that might distract us from our job of objectively examining the specific policies that were implemented and measuring them on their merits.

JD: Yes, I think that's right. It does work better if you're trying to understand how a society is doing politically if you look at the consequences rather than the process. You won't be able to see the processes very well and you can see some of the consequences very easily, so it's a much clearer picture.

And that is the picture that matters: if the processes are very elaborate and very seemly in appearance but the consequences are very bad, that is not good, that's not a good political structure. The point of political institutions isn't to look good, the point of political institutions is to have good consequences.

The law is actually a very important idea here. There are aspects of political institutions which are captured, and probably only potentially capturable, through the idea of a law which is observed and actually provides some range of definite guarantees. It is a virtue of the United States, and its Constitution, that it was established with that idea at its centre—not just at the centre of a set of legal documents but at the centre of a political project.

And although you can't say that Alexander Hamilton actually cared much about that, there were other people around at the time who were involved in designing what occurred who were very centrally concerned with precisely that goal, and they had a remarkable degree of success.

Questions for Discussion:

1. Do you think that a prolonged period of Chinese economic success will make Westerners rethink some aspects of their current governance structure?

2. To what extent is it possible to separate questions of governance, economic management and civil liberties?

VI. India

The world's largest democracy

HB: We've spoken a fair amount about the United States: contemporary United States, historical United States, the idealized version of the United States and so forth. This is, of course, extremely important historically, economically and culturally.

But it could well be that one of the most salient countries to look at when one wants to look at the entire modern project of democracy is not the United States at all, but India, which is certainly the largest democracy that exists today and is arguably a much more surprising development in terms of what they've been able to achieve in erecting a stable, democratic regime that has lasted since independence in 1947.

In light of their tremendous diversity of languages and cultures and traditions and history, I wonder if most people aren't fully appreciating the fact that India should be just as much examined and just as closely regarded—perhaps even more so—than the Unites States to comprehend the impact and the influence of democracy and democratic structures.

What is your view? When you look back at the initial conditions, are you astounded by what has been achieved in India? Do you think that, if we look carefully at India, we'll find lessons for all sorts of other people?

JD: I certainly think that if you look at India you can see things about democracy as a possible political structure, which are much more plausibly relevant to most of the world than what you see if you look at the United States. The Unites States became what it is now under very, very privileged circumstances, which are dramatically unlike those that have been obtained virtually anywhere else.

And that, I think, has given American political comprehension some very serious limitations, because in general Americans don't perceive how far the more attractive features of their political arrangements have depended upon gifts of providence.

If you ask, *What's really good about the United States from a political and social and imaginative point of view?* and *Where has that come from?* it's a mistake to suppose that it has come from a set of very edifying ideas, principally. It's come from a set of remarkably favourable historical circumstances for those who won the near-exterminatory war for control of the current United States landmass.

HB: OK, but let's return to this point that you were making about India and the fact that it may be more germane for the rest of the world because the circumstances that gave rise to the American experiment were so unique. I suppose it could be argued that India was also very fortunate in the choice of its leaders at the time of independence who were particularly cultivated, thoughtful and able individuals, but given the sheer complexities of the place, it's really a wonder that a democratic regime can be as stable and effective as it has been.

JD: Well, I think there are several things you can say about the Indian version of democracy. One is that it illustrates how political relations can be structured and realized under a very wide range of conditions given enough luck. And once it begins to be realized, it can actually build up its own support base.

Democracy can be dismantled anywhere in principle. It would be harder to dismantle it in the United States than most other places, but it could be dismantled anywhere. But if you look at South Asia, it's very striking that it hasn't been dismantled in India. I mean, it has been pretty effectively dismantled in Pakistan—it sort of comes and goes, but it more often goes than comes. It's certainly been very roughed up in Bangladesh, and it's taken a pretty horrendous form in the last 15 or 20 years in Sri Lanka.

In many ways India is a horrible society. It's full of cruelty and ugliness. Of course, it's not one society if you think about it that way, but at any rate what we think of as the current Indian state is not a pretty human picture. It has a very, very deep imaginative background in which people are differentiated by value and by dignity, and in that sense is very drastically inegalitarian and hierarchical.

So you would think—and actually political scientists at the time mostly did think—that a country that poor and that big, which repels the idea of political equality, can't actually sustain representative democratic institutions.

And in many respects, the society *does* repel the idea of political equality by what it is and how it lives, but the state structure is formally a structure of political equality and its institutional forms realize the primal act of political choice that is available in representative democracies. It realizes the free and equal vote. In fact, I would say that it realizes it with a fidelity and comprehensiveness that is certainly not matched by either the United States or the United Kingdom. Indian electoral processes are run to an astonishingly high level. And that is definitely not true of the electoral processes of the United States or the United Kingdom, as some very conspicuous recent examples have drawn to wide attention.

The British and American versions don't realize it to the same extent because they haven't really tried to. They certainly haven't tried to for anything like the same time and with anything like the same degree of commitment, so of course they haven't succeeded.

Now that shows, first of all, that you *can* actually build a state which has at least this aspect of democracy very fully realized in a very, very poor country. You need some facilities to build it through, but it can be done, because it has been done.

Every time there is an Indian general election, there is, broadly speaking, the largest free electoral choice there has ever been in human history. So that's quite something. But there is something else which is also terribly important: in India, through the way in which the legal structure of the state was established and through the political processes that have worked through this structure, there has been a relatively steady erosion of the ugliest forms of social hierarchy.

The caste structure has been politically weakened through democratic institutions and through the development of public law as a result of the electoral decisions. That is definitely, in my view, a process of political correction of some of the worst features about India.

I think that is a very considerable achievement politically and I think that it is owed to democracy. It isn't owed *just* to the idea of democracy, but it's owed to the extent to which the idea of democracy has been realized, at least through the electoral structure in India.

There are no places where what goes on politically is unequivocally positive. That's not what humans are like. It's not what human choices are like *en gros*, and it's not what happens inside the structuring of political institutions.

But the point of trying to make political institutions that achieve good consequences is that they should make those good consequences likelier. And there have been some good consequences of the way Indian democracy has worked, and they are attributable to it being, to that degree, democratic. So there are great achievements in that story.

Question for Discussion:

1. Do you think that the political achievements of democratic India are, broadly speaking, sufficiently recognized throughout the rest of the world?

VII. Power to the People

Overthrowing autocracy and what happens next

HB: Another very positive and inspirational aspect of what most people mean by democracy is this ability to act in opposition to tyranny and autocracy. We've seen one relatively recent manifestation of this in the Arab Spring of 2011.

You point out that one of the singularly great appeals of democracy, certainly in the initial stages, is to act in precisely this way: in opposition to something. And perhaps the most seductive aspect of democracy is inciting people to rise up as a collective voice and overthrow oppressive regimes.

The difficulty, of course, is that once one has done that, it's a rather different kettle of fish to actually develop the sorts of responsible, stable and effective institutions that you were talking about.

JD: Well, I think that the idea of being able to stop yourself being ruled odiously and harmfully is an idea which has an overwhelming political appeal to any possible human population.

And democracy, if it is realized in the institutional forms that we have around here, does at least guarantee that sooner or later you will be able to do that. You will be able to stop yourself being ruled by people whom you see as intolerable.

HB: Sure. You can "throw the bums out".

JD: I think that the appeal of that is essentially the same as the appeal of overthrowing an autocratic regime, but of course the aftermath is more promising in what we think of as a democracy, because it will naturally include as the political outcome the choice of the majority of the population.

If you overthrow an autocratic regime, it's anyone's guess what the outcome is going to be, and pretty much anyone's guess what institutional structures the outcome is going to emerge from. It may emerge from the army. It may emerge from religious seminaries. It might emerge from all sorts of places, but you can't have any degree of rational confidence in its emerging from somewhere that you'd want it to emerge from.

A simple, and intuitively very powerful, merit of representative democracy in its Western form is that it's a strongly institutionalized, and therefore strongly institutionalizeable, way of ensuring that opportunity.

That's a very good opportunity to have; and sooner or later if you don't have it you're going to wish very much that you did have it, and it's going to be potentially very expensive to try to get it.

So democracy is better than revolution because revolution is very dangerous and erratic and extremely likely to end in more tears than joy. Democracy isn't very likely to end in joy either, but it gives joy a better chance.

Questions for Discussion:

1. Do democracies encourage or suppress large-scale public demonstrations?

2. To what extent is a failed revolution more harmful to democratic ideals than no revolution at all?

VIII. Towards Progress

Why we should care about all of this

HB: If I'm a non-specialist who is listening to this, I might think to myself something like, *Here's Professor Dunn. He's a very deep and knowledgeable fellow who's thought very deeply about how society should be ruled, and on which institutions we should depend, and how they might be measured and judged to determine whether or not they are doing so effectively and efficiently. He cares very much about these long-term structural issues. But I have the good fortune to live in a modern democracy, and while I recognize that it's not perfect, and that my version of democracy is not the same as it was in other places at other times, what does all of that really matter? How is all of this relevant to me?*

JD: Well, it's relevant to you because it's part of what's caused the setting in which you live and a lot of the features of that setting, so it's relevant *explanatorily*: if you want to understand what's been going on in your life, you need to understand some of this. You won't understand it unless you do.

Now, lots of people don't particularly want to understand what's been going on in the setting of their life because they are, in a sense, fine with their life. If you're very happy with your circumstances, and you don't particularly care about anything beyond your circumstances, then I don't think you do have a good reason to want to fathom all this.

It's not that easy to fathom, you won't completely succeed in fathoming it, and it won't show you how to transform your immediate personal circumstances for the better. But it depends on what you do care about, and it depends a great deal on how bad the consequences of the way you're being governed at the time are. So you have to think in two different directions to see what all this is about.

First of all, you have to see that, in fact, a very large proportion of what is going on in our social world is dangerous and probably very destructive, very damaging. You have to see that a very great deal of bad is being done all the time, and that bad will certainly affect you negatively in the course of your life.

I have a reasonably good chance of not being very affected by it so much myself because I'm old enough, but one way or the other it will certainly affect my children or grandchildren or great-grand-children. It will affect lots and lots of people.

If you don't care about other people, I suppose you don't need to worry about that. But if you *do* care about them, then without political understanding you can't think about what to try to bring about, you can't think about who you could ally with to try to improve the outcome. In short, you will be completely politically impotent.

It's fine, entirely selfishly, to be completely politically impotent if you're delighted with every feature of your own life and you don't care about anyone else's. And probably if you don't live for very long.

But if you alter any of those conditions, then you're into a space in which it will matter quite a lot, potentially, if what's happening is very bad. It will matter whether or not you understand that it's happening, because of course you can't do anything about it unless you understand what's happening.

And you also won't be able to do much about it if only *you* understand what's happening. These are *political* processes: they involve a very large number of people. My preoccupation is with the question of how it's possible to show people what's happening so that they can decide for themselves what to do about it. They may well decide to do nothing about it for one reason or another, but still they can't decide unless they can see.

HB: So that's a necessary first step. It's necessary to get an appreciation of what exactly the problem is before one goes about trying to actually deal with matters.

But do you have any sense of a possible clear prescription? I don't mean to be overly combative, and I'm not looking for pat, all-encompassing formulae, but it would be nice to be a little more concrete.

JD: There is a formula that I think helps to think about these things because it wakes one up a bit. It comes from an Italian novel called *The Leopard*, which is about *ancien régime* Sicily, Garibaldi and the birth of modern Italy. The hero, who's a grandee, says, *"If things are going to stay as they are, things will have to change."*

That is the central political insight: it is *not safe* for most people unless they care about very little beyond themselves and they don't care much about future time. What is happening is *almost always very bad* from their point of view.

And they can't actually think about what can be done about that unless they think about the political position in which they are situated and what can and can't be done politically through the structures that actually define that position.

If you don't understand politics, you can't have any coherent conception of how the immense damage that human beings have done to the planet on which they live can be brought under minimal control within the foreseeable human future. And if it isn't, then there won't *be* good human lives in a few hundred years. There just won't be able to be.

There are people who say, *"Well, you don't need to worry about these things because we have a reliable magical secret, which will sort out the chaos we make."* And that sort of idea—which is quite an old idea, actually—has different modern representatives. There are those who say, *"Well, we have the magic of the market. That sorts everything out in the end."*

Well, look around.

Or they say, *"Well we have science. That is constituted out of comprehension. The market perhaps isn't."*

The reigning theory of the market at the beginning of 2007 was that the market has perfect comprehension and it works through its perfect comprehension.

HB: Maybe it does, maybe it's just malicious.

JD: Well, that's, as it were, the economic equivalent of natural theology as read by David Hume: perhaps, actually, the world was invented by a completely incompetent and rather malicious deity.

So you can explain the variance through increasing the level of malice or you can explain the variance by increasing the level of incompetence, but you can't explain the horrible mess of the way the world is through the idea that it's all caused by an omnipotent and benevolent creator. That idea just crashes.

Well, the market's just like that. It's like natural theology: you can have what it actually does or you can have a pretty story about it.

Questions for Discussion:

1. Are political structures somehow tied closer to economic structures now than they were 20 or 30 years ago? Will they be even more tied to them in the future?

2. Are there genuine opportunities for individuals, or small groups of individuals, to create large-scale societal impact in contemporary society?

IX. Professional Indulgence
Critically examining "political science"

HB: Let me switch gears a bit, now, and talk a bit about the field of political science proper.

As a non-specialist, I was very gratified when I saw your books, because it was clear that there was a specialist out there who was not only taking these ideas very seriously, but also writing about them for a popular audience.

And listening to you speak so passionately about our need to better understand the problems that are confronting our societies, the need to be able to judge better, the need to be able to learn from our mistakes, to, as it were, change so that we can stay the same, it seems to me that this should be a relatively common theme within the discipline of political science and political theory.

Is it? Is this the sort of thing that many of your colleagues are talking about? Are they also examining democracy with a fine-toothed comb? Are they looking at it with the same level of judgment and keenness that you are? Or are you a bit of an outlier when it comes to this sort of thing? And, if so, why?

JD: Well, I think the sense in which I am a bit of an outlier is really largely a matter of arrogance. I have tried to understand what has been happening through this word "democracy" as a single process through time. That's hardly a popular approach.

There are a few other people who've tried, but they've been sufficiently unsuccessful at doing so that it doesn't really matter whether they've tried.

It's eccentric to try to do anything that is so obviously beyond the reach of any person as that, and it's not well regarded in academic circles to try to do something that you're certainly not going to succeed in. You're supposed to succeed in what you do, and you're supposed to show that you've succeeded incontrovertibly to a professional audience who will instead try to demonstrate that you've fluffed it.

So doing this sort of thing is not the way in which to build a solid academic career. I started doing it, to be frank, after I didn't need to build a career—it was already built and I could do what I liked. I did it because I thought it was very interesting, increasingly interesting as I engaged in it, in fact.

What was true about it was obviously important, and what actually turned out to be true about it was very disconcertingly different from the way people normally see it and speak about it.

But most academics who work on politics, on political theory, on political philosophy, on political sociology, concentrate on what they think are well-defined questions. And they believe that they provide robust and compelling answers to these well-defined questions.

Now, in order to be able to do that with political stuff, you have to pull a long way back from the world. And my general intuitive judgment is that if you pull a long way back from the world of politics, you just lose politics. It's gone.

HB: But what's the point of doing it at all, then? Why do you necessarily have to pull a long way back from the world in political science?

I mean, you may want to create an idealized case or something to begin your analysis, but surely the context of what it is that you're doing should be *all about the world*. It should have something meaningful to say about political systems and the world as we find it. Otherwise it just becomes some abstract academic exercise in self-indulgence, right?

JD: Well, of course the academics wouldn't say that what's going on is self-indulgent...

HB: Of course they wouldn't.

JD: They would say, *"It's demonstrating professional competence to a potentially adversarial audience. And after all, that's the way science works..."*

HB: No. Science describes the world. It doesn't just demonstrate professional competence. I mean you could have professional competence about tiddlywinks—

JD: *"Oh,"* they'd reply, *"Political scientists describe the world..."*

HB: Not the political world.

JD: Well, that's *my* point.

They describe what are specifiable bits of the political world and they describe them in terms in which it's going to be very difficult to show that they've misdescribed them. But in order to do that, they have to stop asking a great many questions about politics, they have to define a potentially controllable subject matter in its defined form that is unproblematically there.

Now once you define something that is unproblematically there, politically, you will have lost politics. Because politics is in the dynamism and unobviousness of what is *actually* there. It's in the chaotic character of human interaction. And you can't capture that through scientifically robust instrumentation. The ideas of scientifically robust instrumentation and capturing politics just aren't reconcilable with one another.

And what has happened in the history of political science, the professionalization of political science, is that a very large majority of those who do political science—even if they're actually very astute about politics in private life and can talk very well about those things they know about it—do something quite different.

What they've ended up doing professionally is actually not to talk very well about politics, but to talk about politics in a way that is not subject to professional criticism.

So they've taken up what's actually a very defensive posture, and a defensive posture that is quite strongly prudentially reinforced.

And they've adjusted to that. I think that most of them don't really recognize the cost they've incurred by doing so.

HB: It seems to me like those costs are enormous.

JD: Well, they're much higher from the point of view of those who aren't political scientist or political theorists than they are for those who are. Because those who are political scientists or political theorists have, in a sense, already budgeted for the costs. In some sense you could say that they've embraced the costs.

HB: Let's look at it from the vantage point of the average person on the street who might start asking these broader questions about what is going on inside universities: *What is a mathematician doing? What is a political theorist for? Why do we have universities?*

From this perspective, one can compare a political scientist with a mathematician. A mathematician—let's say a pure mathematician and not an applied mathematician—is doing highly logically rigorous work within a very abstract domain which generally has no direct relevance whatsoever to human society or the human condition (at least not deliberately).

And then you have the political theorist who is supposed to be discussing things that have overwhelming import to most people—namely human societies: how they're presently structured and how they might be improved. This will likely be very nebulous and not rigorous at all, filled with potential contradictions and interpretations and general messiness—"the chaotic character of human interaction," as you put it a moment ago.

But when we're investigating something like democracy—whether democracy has actually been effective and efficient, how best to enlighten the people who are, at the end of the day, the ones who are involved in the decision procedure of choosing governments—it seems to me that this is of overwhelming import. I guess that's my sense of frustration. We're not just playing some academic game here: we're talking about real people and real societies and real judgments and how to actually make the world a better place.

You talked earlier about ecological catastrophes that we have to avoid, or at least do our best to minimize, there are massive numbers of people around the world whom we'd naturally like to try to elevate from conditions of misery and dire poverty. These are real issues that are of massive import to our societies.

And I'm *hoping*, as someone who is a non-specialist, that people at universities who are doing research in political science are thinking somewhat deeply about these issues and trying to add constructive comments and criticisms and theories so that they can positively influence the way society functions.

But if I become convinced that, at the end of the day, they're just playing some self-consistent, self-referential game where they can publish papers and get these papers judged by fellow colleagues based upon internal sets of criteria and so forth and so on—well, that seems pretty much like a waste of time to me.

JD: Well, I think it *is* rather a waste of time myself, and I also think it's a waste of money. I mean, if you ask, *"Well, who needs political science departments?"* the answer is not so evident. Obviously, political scientists need political science departments. But it isn't unequivocally clear in the case of most political science departments that anyone else actually needs them.

And I think that that's definitely wrong. The fact is people *do* need political comprehension, and the way in which political science has been institutionalized over time is hugely unhelpful—most of it doesn't provide much political comprehension.

And even if you take, as it were, all the best bits of it and you somehow juxtaposed them, you don't end up with a very high level of political comprehension because there is no synoptic capability in that juxtaposition, because there is no synoptic *effort*.

Nobody tries to answer what, after all, in the end is the primary question—and I'm sure, in a sense, is the same question that physicists must be struggling with—which is, *"**What** the hell is really going on, and **why** is it going on?"*

HB: And how can we affect it?

JD: Yes. Well, you aren't going to be able to affect it in any way you want to if you don't know what it really is and you don't understand why it is.

HB: That seems a particularly fitting place to end. Thank you very much, John. It's been a pleasure.

JD: You're very welcome.

Question for Discussion:

1. *In what ways has this conversation impacted your views about democracy, contemporary politics, or the field of political science?*

Continuing the Conversation

Readers interested in John's detailed perspective on these topics are referred to his books, *Setting the People Free: The Story of Democracy*, *Breaking Democracy's Spell* and *Traditionalism: the only radicalism.*

Ideas Roadshow Collections

Each Ideas Roadshow collection offers 5 separate expert conversations presented in an accessible and engaging format.

- *Conversations About Anthropology & Sociology*
- *Conversations About Astrophysics & Cosmology*
- *Conversations About Biology*
- *Conversations About History, Volume 1*
- *Conversations About History, Volume 2*
- *Conversations About History, Volume 3*
- *Conversations About Language & Culture*
- *Conversations About Law*
- *Conversations About Neuroscience*
- *Conversations About Philosophy, Volume 1*
- *Conversations About Philosophy, Volume 2*
- *Conversations About Physics, Volume 1*
- *Conversations About Physics, Volume 2*
- *Conversations About Politics*
- *Conversations About Psychology, Volume 1*
- *Conversations About Psychology, Volume 2*
- *Conversations About Religion*
- *Conversations About Social Psychology*
- *Conversations About The Environment*
- *Conversations About The History of Ideas*

All collections are available as both eBook and paperback.

www.ingramcontent.com/pod-product-compliance
Lightning Source LLC
Chambersburg PA
CBHW030237030426
42336CB00009B/146